THE E-HERO'S GUIDE TO
REAL ESTATE INVESTING

THE E-HERO'S GUIDE TO
REAL ESTATE INVESTING

Increase Your Cash Flow
Without Increasing Your Work Day

BY BRANDON K. MOORE

CONTENTS

CHAPTER 1

INTRODUCTION TO REAL ESTATE INVESTING

The Entrepreneur Real Estate Investor

Lying under the floor of this two-bedroom, one-bath house, I began to rethink my choices. Several questions came to mind.

First, why did I choose to dive headfirst into the crawl space of this pier-and-beam home all alone?

Second, what did I think I would accomplish? I had no tools or real skills in diagnosing or fixing gas or plumbing issues. I'm an accountant, not a carpenter, plumber, or handyman.

Next, why did I buy this house? Yes, I'd imagined myself as a real estate investor, but was this the type of work I should expect from here on out? I'm not claustrophobic, but the darkness, the cold, musty smell, and the spider webs all around me gave me a taste of fear.

I had shimmied headfirst into this space without a shovel or any tool to move dirt around. Now, I was stuck. There was no one to call out to in the house. I was alone with my thoughts—and the spiders.

At the time, I weighed about 140 pounds. At six feet tall, I was skin and bones. With the arm strength of a junior high mathlete, my hope of getting out of this predicament was slim.

I was able to scoot myself towards the hole I had entered several minutes before. Eventually, my hands could reach the floorboards surrounding the hole. After a short prayer, I threw my legs up the hole and pulled on the wooden ridge with everything I had. By the grace of God—and probably with a furious guardian angel—I made it out.

As I again saw the gracious light of day, I reminded myself, *"I'm an accountant! Why the Hell am I climbing into holes?!"*

I wish I could say that was the last time I decided to work on my own properties, but it wasn't. I had to learn some more lessons in repair and remodel before choosing to hang up my tool belt.

This was my first income-producing property—and the beginning of my life as a real estate entrepreneur.

Who Is This Book for?

This book probably isn't for you. I'm sorry. I know that was hard to read. You probably paid for this book thinking it was an answer to your real estate investing needs. Or maybe that you would get some insight into the process and path towards wealth.

Well, it is those things. But more likely than not, it won't work for you. You're not ready. You need to work on some other things first.

What things? you might ask. Well, you need to get your finances in order. You need to pay off some credit cards. Or you have other priorities. Am I right?

When people ask me about investing, if I ask why they haven't started, they give me these excuses. The truth is, they are right. Real estate investing isn't for everyone. It takes discipline and a long-range plan. You can start anytime, but the later you start, the harder it is. And people tend to collect many bad financial habits over a lifetime—which will hinder your success in real estate investing.

Who is this book for? It's for the entrepreneur—or possibly the entrepreneurial-minded person—who has already begun the lifestyle needed to succeed in real estate. Entrepreneurs know what it takes to sacrifice and toil for their business.

I wrote this book for people with the grit to go on Motel 6-and-McDonalds vacations with their kids to save money. They have never, and probably never will, buy a new car. And their house is well below what their earnings would allow. You know who you are. You have a vision and will never sacrifice your future on the altar of the now!

Entrepreneurs are a different subset of the population. Most go through a cycle of love-hate with their businesses which borders on manic-depressive. After a few years, if they haven't lost everything, they've created something that supplies a good living for them and their families.

It is at this point in their lives that my book would be helpful.

Entrepreneurs are always looking for more ways to make money. They need to make more money, because tomorrow isn't guaranteed, and they are compelled to provide for their families beyond today. Then, the issue becomes how to do so without adding another sixty-hour workweek, putting their kids into child labor, or hoping to win the lottery.

Real estate might be the answer.

Who Will You Become?

By following the coaching and instruction in this book, you will become more confident in wading into the river of real estate investment. You will find your path from my mistakes, victories, and lessons learned from the last twenty-plus years of investing. Like Joshua, I want to roll back the Jordan River of confusion or doubt about your ability to buy income-producing property. (See the book of Joshua, chapter three, in the Bible.) But also like Joshua, I can only show you the path. You must choose to take the next steps and walk onto dry ground.

I want this book to prepare you to pull the trigger on your investing career.

It took me a while to pull that trigger, so I'd understand your hesitation. I spent many years asking mentors and clients about investing, without taking that next step. When I did eventually invest in real estate, several of my friends did the same. But some did not.

One particular friend never would take that next step. He was a saver but didn't trust the equity market or real estate market. While I don't judge his hesitancy, I saw the toll this decision took on him. He worked two full-time jobs and almost never saw his family.

There are many such people around. They were told success comes from a steady job and paycheck. Robert Kiyosaki calls that the "rat race" in his well-known book, *Rich Dad, Poor Dad*. This is a race where you work for your money instead of your money working for you.

I understand the rationale that reinforces our status quo, but I also know what's on the other side. I've successfully invested in real estate, and I aim to make it possible for you, too.

From reading my book, I hope that you will have the tools you need to have faith and trust in yourself to step into your real estate investing career.

Who Am I?

As I stated before, I've been investing in real estate for more than twenty years. My company currently owns and manages around eighty-plus single-family homes in West Texas. I'm the CEO and sole shareholder of BKM pc Certified Public Accountants (pc stands for Professional Corporation). As a CPA, I help businesses and individuals earn more and keep more of what they earn. We do this through accounting, tax compliance and planning, business advisory, and business and real estate coaching. I am also a financial advisor with BKM Financial, LLC, offering financial planning, retirement planning, wealth management, investment, and insurance products. You can say that my life's work has been to see entrepreneurs and their families succeed financially.

On the personal side, I am from Irving, Texas, but went to high school at Warrensburg High School in the metropolis of Warrensburg, Missouri. Its claim to fame is "Old Drum," the legendary dog whose court case—after he was shot in 1869 by a livestock farmer—brought about the famous saying, "A dog is man's best friend." As soon as I could, I got back to Texas for college—and to find my beautiful wife, Angela. We have four kids as of 2021, ages ten to twenty-three. I love my family. They are why I work smarter instead of longer.

Real estate made it possible for us to live comfortably, even when my CPA firm was just getting started. As property manager, my wife toted our kids around to show properties, and sometimes they helped her clean and make them ready to rent again. Real estate has always been the "family business" for us.

By the way, since our niche is in single-family residential real estate, I may interchangeably use the terms *property*, *house*, or *home*. You interpret that to the area of real estate investing that most interests you.

So what do I mean by it being our family business? Today, my oldest and only daughter has been my property manager for five years. She began a few months before she graduated from high school. My oldest son worked on our remodel crew—and then ran that crew. My middle son is learning to remodel and has begun to mow lawns for the vacant properties. He says he's having fun! My youngest is just ten years old, so it will be a few years before he gets involved.

This book was born out of my desire to leave my kids a manual and history of our real estate experience. Because of our deep desire to see entrepreneurs gain and keep their wealth, you, the *hero entrepreneur*, also have become my audience.

Who is the E-Hero?

The purpose of this book is to guide the entrepreneur in building up his real estate empire. Entrepreneurs already possess the discipline and courage to venture out into the real estate world. With the right guidance, you too can become a real estate entrepreneur.

Like I stated in my book, *The E-Hero's Journey: Your Guide to the Entrepreneur Quest*, this journey is full of internal and external obstacles. But you are the *E-Hero*! You are well able to fight through and conquer this quest!

Which Way Forward from Here?

In 2009—in San Angelo, Texas, in my living room—my closest friend at the time, Pastor Brandon Clark, started Celebration Church of San Angelo. He believed that their mission was to help people know God and trust him more. At the beginning of that church plant, one of his favorite sayings was, "Which way forward from here?" It was a reflective question designed to bring comfort.

You see, you are always moving—either towards good things or not-so-good things.

If you were in the seats of the rented movie theater in the church plant's beginnings and hadn't known anything about God—or if you had been a Christian for years—the question "Which way forward from here?" applied to you.

I have used that question in coaching meetings and discussions with friends and family. I feel that it just pegs us in a spot and forces us to look ahead and decide what our next steps will be.

As you consider your way forward, I hope that you will read this book and learn something new. Just as I've shared, and as I will explore more, I took a while to pull the trigger and buy my first property. I hope you choose to take your next steps; don't wait any longer!

CHAPTER 2

MAKING MONEY IN REAL ESTATE

Cash Flow Versus Taxable Net Income

When I started buying investment real estate, we had only months before purchased our first home. It was a HUD foreclosure that we had bid on and won.

When my wife saw it for the first time, she cried. It was unlivable. My father-in-law, Larry Lane, took a week off work, and we busted our tails to get the place livable.

I had just graduated from college with my accounting degree and was working as a tax preparer/staff accountant for a one-CPA accounting firm. My interest in real estate began when I found out that one of our pastors at church was a real estate agent and owned about twenty-five properties.

I admired this pastor—Darrel, the Indiana Jones of ministry. As the missions pastor, he had so many stories about taking the gospel to hostile areas. When I learned that he had invested in real estate to help finance his mission trips, I probably annoyed him with questions about rental properties for two to three years. He was very gracious in helping me understand the industry.

When we finally bought our first property, 417 Howard Street, for $26,400, it was purchased from Pastor Darrel. He gave me a fantastic deal, and I don't remember if he even took the typical commission from the sale.

We bought the property using financing through a local bank with a special "no money down" program. (Those don't exist much anymore.) I didn't have any cash and even put the earnest money amount on a credit card. (Do not do this. Cash advances are extortion!)

Pastor Darrel called. "Bring $400 in a cashier's check on the day of the closing," he told me. *Gulp.* I didn't have it and couldn't borrow it.

When I hung up the phone, I began to pray. The title company was only a few blocks from my office, so I walked to the closing when it came time. Before making the trek, I called Angela, who was supposed to meet me there.

"We need $400 to bring to the closing," I told her, not needing to explain why this was a concern.

"What are we going to do?" she asked.

"Pray," I answered simply. "And I'll do the same." This wasn't the first—or last—time that prayer was my answer to a challenging situation.

Nor was it the first or last time that my prayers would be answered.

When I showed up at closing, I'm sure I was sweating. Upon entering the doors of the title company, Pastor Darrel immediately apologized.

"I am sorry, Brandon. I told you to get a cashier's check. I read the closing statement wrong, and *they* owe *you* $400."

Sighing in relief, I smiled. "That's good," I admitted, "because I didn't have it! I figured y'all would laugh at me and tell me to get lost, or we would walk out with the keys."

Within the next month, we had our first tenant. We received his deposit and first month's rent one day before the first payment was due—like clockwork. We felt the reward for *moving forward.*

Real estate investing is not for everyone, but for those who want to jump in, there are many ways people can make money. So let's dive into some important concepts.

What is the difference between cash flow and net income? As a business owner, I know that *cash is king.* Most small business owners use the "checking account method" of measuring their business success. If there is cash in the account, they feel good; if there isn't, they feel bad. But there is more to it than that.

Net income is the difference between gross revenues and expenses. Is that the same as cash flow? Not exactly. Some non-cash expenses can show up on a profit and loss statement, while not reducing cash. Alternatively, there are cash disbursements that do not count against gross revenue when calculating net income. For example, with note payments to the bank for your equipment loan, you report the interest on the profit and loss statement as an expense, but the principal portion of the payment does not get reported.

So what does this mean in real estate? For a real estate investor who is looking to rent a single-family residence, cash flow is what matters. The net income from operating a rental business—and how you are taxed—is for you to discuss with your tax advisor. But the important thing to remember here is that you want cash flow.

Cash Flow

There are three main objectives when investing in real estate: *cash flow*, *appreciation*, and *ordinary income*.

First, as discussed, is *cash flow*, which we will discuss as being on a monthly basis.

When we started, my father-in-law and I had created the Lane Family Partnership. His last name was Lane, and since he only had girls, I thought naming it after him would keep his namesake going. He had worked in the grocery business for thirty years. Over that time, the store he worked for had sold maybe four times. Each time it sold, he would cash out his retirement account to pay down debt or remodel his house.

This isn't a good practice, and the net result was that at age fifty-eight he only had a little more than $6,000 in his retirement account.

When he approached me to go into business together, he did have a duplex that he had purchased. He and my mother-in-law lived on one side while his aging mother-in-law lived in the other side.

At the time, his equity in the duplex—the fair market value minus the amount he owed the bank—was over $70,000. He decided to refinance the property and pull out $50,000 to start our partnership.

I had two properties that I had already purchased as rentals with a little bit of equity, so we put all of that together into the new entity. We bought several properties from Larry's $50,000 cash investment and eventually created cash flow for him during his retirement.

For rentals, cash flow is the gross rent less the mortgage payment (if any). For example, if your mortgage payment is $1,000 per month, and you receive $1,750 per month in rent, your cash flow on that property is $750. Note that I generally refer to that as the *gross cash flow*. *Net cash flow* also considers the real estate taxes, insurance, management fees, utilities, and a repair allowance—which are important components to address.

When we talk about evaluating property, I will get more detailed about these expenses and the required cash flow targets. I like to see 40 to 50 percent gross cash flow and 20 to 40 percent net cash flow before I will consider buying a property.

Within the category of rent income, there are several options for the real estate investor. My preferred method is a single-family residential rental. You can also invest in commercial rentals, storage units, multi-family apartment complexes, vacation homes (VRBOs), and hotels. It is essential to investigate the various types of rental income and then find your niche.

We have chosen single-family homes because it is a category we know a lot about, and it seems to work for us. You might find the commercial rental space is what works for you. Even though most of what I will tell you is for the single-family space, that doesn't mean it won't relate to other niches.

Appreciation Value Methods

The second objective is *appreciation value*. For tax purposes, residential real estate depreciates over 27.5 years. That means that part of the cost of the property (3.63% per year) is expensed every year, which lowers the "book value" of the property. But in truth, real estate appreciates over time. How does this work?

Roy Rogers said, "You should buy land, because God isn't making any more of it." That's why real estate usually increases in value over time.

Years ago, when we moved to the North Austin area in Texas, we looked around to assess the market. It was interesting to visit with real estate agents and review some available properties there. Many investors would rent their properties and take a loss each month in cash flow. We couldn't believe it! But in digging deeper, we found out about Austin's rapid growth and the demand for property there.

Demand creates shortages, and those shortages push the price of real estate upward. Let's say I bought a property for $100,000 in January of 2000. After five years, I expect that property to be worth more than $100,000. In some markets, it may be worth $110,000. In markets like North Austin, that same property may be worth $150,000 or more. So, where the market may not sustain good cash flow, it may produce better appreciation. Which if you're losing $200 a month for five years, totaling $12,000 in losses, you may be willing to take that loss for the $50,000 appreciation increase in value. Most investors would be very willing to take that risk.

Ordinary Income

The third objective of real estate is creating *ordinary income*. Creating ordinary income doesn't necessarily come from an "investment" in real estate. Investing in real estate means that you hold the real estate for more than twelve months. Ordinary income from real estate occurs when whatever method you use happens within a twelve-month span or less. I don't think the scope of this book will include all ways to create ordinary income from real estate, but I'll name a few of those methods here.

First, what has gotten a lot of attention in the last few years is flipping houses. Flipping houses is where you buy a house that is distressed but in a good area, with comparable sales in the same area being substantially higher than the price at which you purchased the flip house.

There's a lot of risk in flipping houses. Remodeling houses always turns up unexpected expenses. Sometimes those unexpected expenses blow up your budget and cause you to take a loss when you sell.

When you flip a house, generally, you buy the house and sell the house within a few months' time. For tax purposes, this is ordinary income and taxed at higher ordinary income tax rates compared to capital gains tax rates.

If you own a house for twelve months or longer and then sell the house, you qualify for capital gains tax rates. These rates are much lower than ordinary income tax rates.

Note that this discussion is not about your personal residence. I agree with Robert Kiyosaki, author of *Rich Dad Poor Dad*, that a personal residence is not an investment. So, flipping houses is more like an occupation or a vocation than an investment. It can be a lot of fun and very lucrative.

We have flipped several houses over the years. Some houses we purchase for flipping, and other houses we convert from rental to a flip house. In that last circumstance, if we held the house for more than twelve months, it would qualify for capital gains tax. There is a caveat. Any depreciation taken as a rental would be recaptured as ordinary taxable income on the sale and taxed at a flat twenty-five percent.

Let's explain the "CPA jargon" here. Recapture means taxing part of the gain differently. As a rental you get to take part of the cost of the house as an expense every year (remember 3.63% for a single-family residence). If after four years you have taken $6,000 as depreciation expense, lowering your taxable income in those years, when you sell, $6,000 of the gain is then taxed at the flat twenty-five percent.

Wholesaling: Earnest Money Option Contracts

Yet another way to make money in real estate but still create ordinary income, more like options trading than investing, is through *wholesaling*. For instance, a person may see a house in a good area that needs a lot of work and then contact the owner and get a contract or the exclusive right to purchase that house for the next thirty to ninety days. Then that person might take that contract and market the property to an investor.

The contract may have cost as little as $100. That's called *earnest money*. An *earnest money contract* is the exclusive right to purchase a piece of property for a set period. Suppose the individual who is the contract holder does not find a buyer within the specified period. In that case, he can either purchase the property himself at the agreed-upon price or let the contract expire, thereby losing the earnest money.

If he chooses to buy the property, the earnest money is applied to the purchase price of the house. If, however, the individual finds an investor who is willing to buy the property, generally, he will sell the property to the investor for an amount over his agreed-upon purchase price with the property owner. At closing, there will be a same-day purchase and sale of the house to the investor from the original owner with the holder of the earnest money contract in between.

For example, John finds a house and contacts the owner of the house. The owner agrees to sell the house for $50,000 to John. The contract is for thirty days, and the earnest money used to secure the contract is $500. John finds an investor who is willing to purchase the house for $65,000. The closing date is set to close within the contract period. On the same day, the owner sells the house to John, and John sells the house to the investor.

John, the wholesaler, nets $15,000 minus any document fees. This income to John is ordinary income. John created something of value when he created the earnest money contract.

Note that it is in John's best interest to make the contract sixty days or more to find an investor and set the closing date within the contract period. Wholesalers must know several investors so that they can successfully market the contract in the specified time.

Seller-Financing

Yet another way to make money in real estate is using *seller-financed notes*. This method accomplishes all three objectives for the investor: cash flow, appreciation, and ordinary income.

The "sale" of the house on a note creates a short-term or long-term capital gain (appreciation), the interest income recognized over the term of the note creates ordinary income, and since you are collecting payments over time, there is monthly cash flow until the buyer pays off the note.

Here's how it works. An investor buys a property, repairs or remodels, then sells the house to a buyer on a note, or a seller financed real estate lien-note sometimes called a mortgage loan.

This is, however, a little more difficult now because of the Dodd-Frank Act, which requires any investor who sells more than five houses per year to become a licensed mortgage loan originator. I will not go into my deep hatred for this act here. I will say that it is not surprising that the American Banking Association helped to write the law, which secured their members as the only entities available to act as lender for these mortgages. In the guise of assisting unsuspecting, low-income home buyers, they have made it harder for people in low-income areas to buy good-quality homes.

That said, you can make money on the sale—and from the interest income from—seller-financed mortgage notes. If you don't want to hold the note, you can sell "paper" to another investor. For example, I bought a house, remodeled it and then sold it to an individual on a seller financed thirty-year note. In the second or third year, I need some extra cash. The balance of the note owed to me is $100,000. I might sell that note to another investor for $95,000. If my original profit was $30,000, when I sold the note, I still made a good amount of profit after selling the note at a "discount." There's a good market for those who buy and sell these notes.

A more complex system of investing in real estate—seller-financing—creates some issues in financing future real estate purchases, because only the gross profit percentage of principle is taxed, not all its cash flow appears on the annual tax return.

Other Income Methods

Real estate development is a lucrative field, although sometimes speculative in nature. For the scope of this book, development won't be included in the discussion of real estate investing; however, I did want to address it here.

Real estate development is where you buy a property, vacant lot, or long-term lease and construct residential or commercial (or a combination of both) units on the site. The units can be sold or rented after completion, and then the developer moves on to the next project. Think Donald Trump before he became president and star of *The Apprentice*.

In the sense that the developer buys property, remodels, and sells or leases, yes, they are an investor. Most of the time, though, the developer takes commissions on the sale of units, fees for construction, and possibly fees for management of the property. Once complete, they are acting in a trade or business, which creates ordinary income.

Becoming a Real Estate Agent

Like Pastor Darrel, some investors choose to get their real estate agent's license. It isn't required to invest, but it may have some advantages.

The disadvantages may outweigh the benefits if you rely on real estate agents to find additions to your inventory. The downside to having your license is that you will be less likely to have other real estate agents bring you potential properties.

They might be hesitant to share commissions with you on the purchase. Also, they know that they will not get the referral when it comes time to sell a property.

Being a real estate agent is a relationship business. We will talk more about the agent-investor relationship in the next chapter. Earning commissions on real estate transactions is ordinary income and doesn't qualify as investing.

If your job is being a real estate agent, why would you *not* invest in real estate as well? You get a first look at MLS listings, and you can usually save money on the purchase and sale. You must decide if getting your license will be more advantageous, or if using excellent investor-focused real estate agents would be better.

Other things to consider around obtaining your real estate license are the need for continuing education, license and MLS fees, and professional liability insurance, often called errors and omissions insurance. I thought about getting my license for a while, and I even started the pre-licensing education courses. I concluded that if I were the agent, that would lock me into who my agent was going forward (me!). If I wanted to change agents and fire myself, I would have paid all the real estate agent expenses for no apparent reason. So, I chose to open my options to some of the best agents in the business in my area— sometimes even having them compete for my business. Also, we have developed friendships with agents over the years that I wouldn't ever want to lose.

Knowing the various ways to make money in real estate gives you many options. You should know and be proficient in more than one method but have one primary vein. For example, you could become an expert at flipping houses or buying apartment complexes for rental income.

As I've shared, our primary revenue stream is the rental of single-family houses. Even so, we sometimes schedule one to four flip houses—either from our current inventory or a house that we buy just for the flip. We do this for several reasons.

One, it's fun to flip houses. Even with all the TV shows on HGTV and A&E that create drama and demonstrate cost overruns, it still feels good to take something ugly and make it beautiful. The transformation is extremely rewarding.

Second, the business sometimes needs the cash infusion. It is an excellent bonus to have a few flips per year to pay for vacations or one of the kids' college tuitions.

Lastly, our maintenance crew is also our remodel crew, and they love to do flips and show off their skills. For rental properties, we don't do custom materials. For flips, however, we let our guys loose to be creative. My daughter and wife also love the design aspect of flips, and it shows.

As we move into the next few chapters, you will understand the groundwork to becoming a real estate investor. Knowing the ways to make money in real estate is just the beginning. Next, we will discuss the crucial members of your real estate advisory team. Yes, real estate investing is a team sport.

CHAPTER 3

GATHERING YOUR TEAM

The Team of Advisors

"Plans fail for lack of counsel, but with many advisors,
they succeed." —Proverbs 15:22 NIV

I didn't play sports in high school or college. I had two things
working against me in that arena.

One, when I began high school, I was only five feet, three
inches tall. I probably weighed in at about 90 pounds soaking
wet. While my other friends had their growth spurts in the
eighth grade, I had yet to grow much.

Second, I had asthma. I loved football, basketball, and
baseball, but since I couldn't run as was needed in basketball,
football and baseball were my sports of choice in junior high.
During football season, I had to tie my inhaler on a string to
my uniform pants. It wasn't a well-engineered plan since I
would land on it painfully if I ever got hit.

When I graduated to high school, I just gave up on sports altogether. I quit baseball because of family issues and have regretted never trying out since.

What I did instead during high school was theater arts. Our one-act play was the closest thing we had to a team. I didn't score the leading role my junior or senior year, but I did get a supporting role. It was my favorite part of high school.

Right before the theater conference tournament, our team received devastating news. Chad Wilson's father had passed away; Chad was the lead role. We were overwhelmed with grief for our teammate. We were all prepared to sit out that tournament. To our surprise, Chad walked into the school, ready to get on the bus and perform. He said that it meant too much to everyone to sit out. He couldn't let us down. Of course, it would not have let any of us down. Sometimes those things happen, and you just have to be mature enough to move forward. But he didn't think about himself; he was thinking about the team. Even though he was filled with grief, he pressed on for us.

I think about that sometimes when I feel overwhelmed. Chad needed us that day, and we needed him. We couldn't perform without him. It seemed he couldn't grieve without us.

I am going to shock you with the following statement: I do not know everything! I'll give you time to pick yourself up off the floor...I know your head is still spinning, but I will go on writing. I have been blessed to have multiple advisors available to me over the years. Similarly, you must have a team of advisors around you in any business that you undertake. We will explore the advisory roles you may want to fill, formally or informally.

The Mentor

Like Pastor Darrell, there may be others in your life who have done what you want to do. They are a great resource.

Most real estate investors love to talk about their experiences. Most would sit down with you and chat, if you are respectful of their time and space out your appointment requests.

Before starting the Lane Family Partnership, Pastor Darrell, my first mentor, had to move, and I needed a new mentor. My goal was one hundred houses, and I needed someone who had an inventory at least twice that of Pastor Darrell. After some job and city changes of my own, I ended up back in San Angelo working for a CPA firm with a good amount of real estate clients. One of those clients was Max Jacobs.

Max is a retired captain from the United States Air Force and has an engineering degree. He was from New York, but after being stationed in San Angelo, Texas, he decided to retire there.

Max is a deal maker. He is always on the lookout for new opportunities to make money. From real estate to options trading, from oil transportation to retail auto shops, he finds money in all the right places.

When I first met Max, he had more than fifty houses. He and his partner, Jim Wade, had several homes in a small housing addition outside of town, and several places spread out over San Angelo.

Max is a very chill, laid-back kind of guy. He would be a great mediator, since he is very empathetic and wise. Also, he is excellent at seeing opportunities as they present themselves.

I don't know if Max knew he was mentoring me. I was a staff accountant tasked with preparing his tax returns, so asking questions was part of the job. Every now and again, I would ask a real estate financing question or ask why he chose to do a transaction a certain way—gaining from him as much as he was willing to share.

In your search for a mentor, you don't need to call someone and ask, "will you be my mentor?" like you were asking someone to go steady. Really, the key is finding that person who has been where you want to go.

The process is similar to asking for recommendations in travel. If you are going somewhere new and need help finding the best restaurant, hotel, or other entertainment, you would ask someone who has been there before.

You can have many mentors at the same time. It is best not to annoy the mentor with questions to get a feel for whether they enjoy the interaction. Just because they enjoyed the first interaction doesn't mean they will always feel that way or feel that way each time you ask. Asking as the need arises helps keep the badgering to a minimum.

Pastor Darrell got tired of my questions when it appeared that they were just research and not applied to a task. When asking Max for help in a particular transaction, however, he seemed to thrive at advising me.

Mentoring isn't the same as coaching. I need to put that here, because there have been many books and management tools developed around coaching. I am a business coach and have coached hundreds of business owners in their specialized industries. As I have said before, I don't know everything. Coaches don't need to have experience in the area they coach. A mentor, on the other hand, is someone who has experience *doing the stuff.* Both have value.

Coaches help you discover the answers on your own, developing creativity in your thinking. A coach doesn't need to have been a tenured investor to know how to ask good questions and encourage you.

Mentors are needed when no amount of self-reflection or questioning will get to the answer. They know the details of the situation, because they have done it. In specific circumstances, they may actually know the people, bankers, real estate agents, sellers with whom you are dealing.

I had a situation where the city wanted to purchase one of my properties. They didn't want the houses themselves; they would just bulldoze them. They wanted the lots. After talking to Max, I knew what had happened in other situations, both good and bad. Also, I received the contact information of house movers. I ended up selling the lots to the city at 120 percent of their value, moving the houses and setting them up on new lots, and getting financing for the new lots and house move. Nothing came out of my pocket, and I kept the gain from the sale.

Finding the right mentor will help you go to the next level. Consider them part of your team. Mentors should positively influence your growth, stretch your idea of success, and challenge your goals. They shouldn't be negative, always tell you *why it won't work,* or be your competitor.

The Real Estate Agent

The next member of your team to seek is an investment-oriented real estate agent. The right real estate agent can make a huge difference in what properties you see, how the negotiations go, and possibly the eventual sale of investment properties.

Some real estate agents only work with homeowners. Working with homeowners is very different than working with investors. Those who only work with homeowners are hesitant about submitting offers that might be lower than the market. Those real estate agents are justified in their hesitation.

However, to do well in real estate, you must get the lowest price on the purchase. The saying goes, "You make your money on *the purchase*." Which is to say, once you purchase the property, you can't change how much you have in it except by increasing it. This sets limits on your profit. Finding the right real estate agent who will help you negotiate the best acquisition price is therefore essential.

Look for somebody who has worked with investors before. Talk to those other investors and ask them who they use. I once had a real estate agent that every time she called, I bought a property. She knew exactly what I wanted and exactly which properties would make money. I don't know why she called me and not the other investors, or just bought the property herself, but I am thankful that she did.

When she passed away, it was very sad for her and her family. I had heard that she had accumulated over one hundred houses in her own inventory. What a remarkable testimony of her life.

So, what is an investor looking for in a real estate agent? There are four key factors that I look for in a real estate agent.

One, they must know the market. Not only the retail market, but they should know the investment property market. There is an investor "discount" that is unspoken. Just think, *less than retail.* How much less depends on the seller and the performance of the real estate agent. Since investors are not emotionally tied to the property, they can and will walk away from negotiations. Your real estate agent needs to know this and be prepared for it.

Second, they must know the rental market. I am a cash flow investor. I want to make monthly cash flow on the property. The market rental value of the property determines your maximum cash flow. What are the top and bottom ends of the rental spectrum? An excellent place to start is with the local housing authority. They have a list of maximum rents for Section Eight housing based on the number of bedrooms and bathrooms. A real estate agent with access to the Multiple Listing Service (MLS) rents for the area is a terrific resource to the investor.

The third factor that a real estate agent needs to know and understand is how financing affects cash flow—what the local market will support for each housing area. Some real estate agents post this info in their marketing package for a property or group of properties. If the 20 percent down, thirty-year amortization doesn't allow for cash flow, I don't want the property. I may not put 20 percent down, but I use a conventional loan estimate when I evaluate the cash flow. In smaller markets, I prefer a fifteen-to-twenty-year amortization period. If you can manage cash flow with a fifteen-year amortization, you should absolutely do so. Every year, your net worth increases by the amount of principal you pay down and any appreciation in the property's value. The shorter the financing term, the faster your net worth grows. We will talk more about financing in later chapters. If a real estate agent keeps bringing me houses that won't produce cash flow, we probably won't work with that agent very long.

The last factor in determining if we will work with a real estate agent is whether they know me and what I am looking for. This is a matter of personal taste. A property can be within all the cash flow stats, but the location or type of house just might not fit our model. Other chapters will discuss finding and evaluating property while having an entrepreneurial mindset with a business model. It is essential to know what you are looking for and have a real estate agent who will listen to and understand you.

Later, after tragically losing the real estate agent I mentioned, I found another who was new in the industry and hungry to make commissions. She would submit my offers, without ever questioning me first, because she didn't know the low-ball offers could be offensive to the sellers.

You shouldn't be concerned with offending the sellers. Often, I inquire of the listing agent how the sales price was determined. I listen for keywords like "comparable sales" and "market value." That almost always means the real estate agent set the price. I have found that some sellers would be delighted with lower amounts, but they let the real estate agent set the price because they "know what it's worth."

When building up my inventory, my philosophy was to put as many offers out as possible and see who responded. Sometimes I would submit ten offers in one week. Many times, I would only get only one response—not an acceptance, but a response. That's all I look for. It means the seller is open to negotiation.

When I do get an acceptance, it is substantially lower than the market value.

One time, my system backfired. I put in ten offers, but five came back accepted! I wasn't ready to buy five houses at once. But with the help of my next team member, I was able to complete the purchases.

The Banker

The next member of your team should be your banker. It is getting more and more difficult to have a relationship with a lender who makes lending decisions. The distance between the person you talk to at the institution and the committee or person who makes the decision may be three levels.

With mortgage companies, you have a mortgage broker who shops several lenders, and then once they find one, they must deal with the underwriting group. There may be a loan officer, a branch manager, and a loan committee or underwriting committee in larger banks.

Whatever your situation, you will want to have someone in your corner who is fighting for you. For our purposes, we will just call this person *the banker*.

The banker will collect your information regarding your finances, your tax returns, your work history, and anything else necessary in the application process. As your banker, they will need to know everything about your financial life. *It is a financially intimate relationship.*

Some people try to hide things from their banker. I don't recommend that. The banker has expertise in finance. They can see whether this venture that you're about to embark on is going to work. If they don't have all the information, they may tell you that it will work, when if the truth were known, it might be evident that it won't. They need to know *all* of your income streams and *all* of your cash disbursements.

The bank is more concerned with cash flow than either a taxable income or a profit and loss statement showing net income. For several years, and because of the complexity of our tax returns, I often created various spreadsheets that helped show my true cash flow. One of these spreadsheets took my taxable income from my tax return and added back all the non-cash deductions that were taken. Also, because we owner financed some properties, we had to add back receipts of principal that were received in cash but not reported as income on my tax return.

When dealing with bankers, honesty is the best policy. Some enlightened bankers will help you identify what needs to be done to qualify for a loan on a new property. Or they may help you understand what the underwriters are looking for in the loan application process.

In our career with real estate, we did have several bankers that told us no to our loan requests. It happens—even when we know the cash flow is there, and the investment is sound.

When that happens, find a new banker. It's best to ask other real estate investors who they use to finance their properties. These recommendations can often come with an introduction. I am grateful for the investors who introduced me to the one or more bankers willing to take on our loan request.

When we first started, I called several of the banks in our town and asked what their loan programs were for investment property. I created a spreadsheet that listed the bank's name, the terms that they were offering for their best loan programs, and their current best interest rate. Sometimes, banks with the lowest down payment requirements had higher interest rates but were easier to work with. I found that the best banks to work with were often charging a little more on their interest rates.

When you're trying to build your inventory, buying the property at a reasonable price is the most critical factor. Interest rates can be changed, either by refinancing or rates changing in the overall market. We used one bank for most of our purchases, and within months, we would refinance to another bank with a lower interest rate. Why would we do this? The first bank allowed us to purchase the property with very little upfront money. Then we might put some money into the property to remodel it. After the remodel, the property would appraise for more than what we purchased it for, and then we could refinance it and get our remodel money back. This is called BRRR or Buy, Rehab, Rent, and Refinance. At the end of the second transaction, we basically purchased the property with no out-of-pocket cash tied up. So, you can see how sometimes the higher interest rate is irrelevant.

A banker or several bankers are an essential part of your real estate investment team. Let's move on to the next member of our team.

The Certified Public Accountant (CPA)
First, you should know that I am a CPA, certified public accountant, as I've shared. If you are not a CPA, more importantly, a tax CPA, you definitely need a CPA on your team. The

enlightened CPA will help you determine the best tax structure and entity choice to operate your real estate investment business.

As a CPA, I had an advantage over other real estate investors. It is probably one of the more expensive members of your team. However, if a good CPA can save you several thousands of dollars per year in tax, they are worth the few thousands of dollars you will spend. I know that sounds a little self-serving, but it is the truth.

If you don't want to take my word for it, you should read *Rich Dad Poor Dad* by Robert Kiyosaki or *The Millionaire Next Door* by Dr. Thomas Stanley. Both discuss the need for and the value of an enlightened CPA.

Not all CPAs are alike. It may take a few interviews and comparing tax years to find the right CPA for your real estate investment needs. Again, this is an excellent time to talk to other real estate investors and ask who they use. Feel free to look my firm up at www.bkm-cpa.com. We work with small business owners and entrepreneurial real estate investors all over the country. We are a completely virtual CPA firm as well!

You should know that a CPA is there to help you reduce your tax liability **and** avoid penalties. I have seen many tax returns improperly prepared that could have created substantial penalties for the taxpayer.

Most real estate investors begin as "do-it-yourself-ers." They are the property manager, repairman, and even the tax preparer. I get it. Why pay someone else when you can do it yourself?

The answer is quite simple. Where you might prepare one tax return per year and see a limited scope of transactions, your CPA sees thousands per year. When you see an experienced quarterback playing in the Super Bowl, and it's almost like he knows what's going to happen before it happens, it's because he has probably seen that exact scenario a hundred times. The value of experience cannot be understated, and it is worth paying for.

As a young investor and CPA, I had other CPAs as my mentors and tax advisors. My advantage as an investor was not that I didn't need advice; I had those around me with more experience who gave me that advice without compensation. In my case, it was considered training for my job. I needed to know this information to better serve my clients. I was just also able to use this information in my investing career.

The Attorney

The next member of your team isn't necessarily a regular member, but it is an important one nonetheless. The real estate attorney is helpful in many areas of real estate investing.

There are countless times in my career when I have needed a real estate attorney—such as with evictions, foreclosures, bankruptcies of tenants, and disputes over property lines. A transaction may be handled by my property manager or myself, but not until after consulting with my attorney. I've had the benefit of a good friend and one of the kindest people I've ever met to be my real estate attorney, W. Hampton Beesley, III. Because of my many mistakes, he has had a lot to do to help me clean up some messes. Usually, documents are out of order, filings are missed, or some other detail must happen before a transaction occurs. I am thankful for what my friend has done for me.

As I wrote this chapter, we became aware that he had passed away. Words cannot express how much I appreciated his influence and kindness.

If you have read Donald Trump's, *The Art of the Deal*, you might think that you need several attorneys on retainer to do anything in real estate. That isn't true. But what is true, if you work in this industry for long, is this: at some point, someone will threaten to sue you. As in any business, it helps to have a relationship with an attorney who specializes in your industry. I can't discuss specific times where Hamp helped us out of a jam; however, I can tell you he did, and I am thankful. He always said he was giving me a discount. I'm not sure if that was true or not. It didn't matter. I valued him and what he did for me.

I once bought a group of fourteen houses from a lady whose son had been her property manager, but he had left the area to go to law school. She didn't want the burden of managing the property any longer. She selected another attorney, not Hamp, to do the closing. I had never been more frustrated with a closing. He had papers everywhere on his conference table, and it was such a mess. After the closing, we had to go back and file corrected deeds for a few of them. This was just fourteen properties. He made so many mistakes, some of which we didn't find until six years later. That process made me appreciate Hamp so much more.

Also, Hamp was such a joy at closing. He always said he did "happy work." In real estate, the buyer and seller are usually happy. That's what he loved, and it showed.

Many attorneys get a bad reputation, but I believe the real estate attorney is a valuable member of your team. There will never be another Hamp, but I will need to find another real estate attorney. My team isn't complete without one.

We've now covered the members of your team that are necessary to begin a career in real estate investment. If you just want to have one or two rental homes, gathering a team might not be as important. But suppose you intend to have a *real estate empire*. In that case, you cannot do without a trailblazing *mentor*, a great *real estate agent*, a creative *banker*, an enlightened *CPA*, and an invaluable *attorney*.

CHAPTER 4

ADOPTING AN ENTREPRENEURIAL MINDSET

Start with Why

I've heard so many stories from so many people as to why they no longer own rental properties. One of my favorites involves a potbelly pig. You read that right!

People in the South sometimes keep potbelly pigs as pets. I was working for a multi-millionaire as a bookkeeper during college. At seventy-eight-ish, He mainly wanted someone to talk to. I was hired to reconcile his bank accounts, about six of them, and to make sure his bonds paid the interest they were supposed to when they were supposed to. He was one of my favorite people.

We talked about how I wanted to invest in rental properties someday, when he told me his tragic story of the potbelly pig. Just after he had purchased some duplexes, a young couple with several kids moved in to one of his properties with their pets. One of those pets was a potbelly pig. Everything in the duplex was new, including the carpet.

Eventually the tenants had financial trouble, and he had to evict them. That is bad enough for your first rental experience. But later, when he went to look over the unit with a handyman, he discovered what a potbelly pig will do. "That pig," he said in disbelief, "got its snout under the edge of the carpet by the kitchen and had run its nose from one end of the duplex to the other, tearing the carpet in half!" That was enough for him. He was done with rentals from then on. He sold the duplexes and never looked back!

I've heard hundreds of stories like this one. All of these stories are meant to deter the average person from engaging in rental real estate. It is true. Real estate investing is not for the faint of heart. The ones who begin the journey by accident or "just test the waters" are the ones who fail or hate the endeavor.

If you are going to be a real estate investor, you need to have an *entrepreneurial mindset*. What do I mean? You must operate as a business. There must be systems and processes in place. You need to have a strategy, mission, vision, and know your customer. Otherwise, you will be flying by the seat of your pants. When something goes wrong, and it most definitely will, you will take it personally! You will resent your tenants and despise the first of the month when they call with excuses or want to chat.

Real estate cannot be a "hobby" and absolutely should not be an afterthought.

Simon Sinek wrote a book called *Start with Why*. It is a great book; you should get it and read it. I'll wait...Okay, so why do you want to invest in real estate? Retirement? Cash flow? Build net worth? Provide housing for seniors? Provide housing for students? All of these are good reasons to invest in real estate. What is *your* reason?

This is the *purpose* or *mission statement* of most businesses. It is the reason why you sacrifice your weekends to install a water heater. It will be the reason you take a risk with a tenant or increase your debt load so much that you have to eat ramen for a month. If you know and have a firm belief behind the *why*, you will endure during the hard times.

As I said before, and as the beginning example illustrates, there will be hard times. I don't know how many times I've just wanted to cash out and leave the real estate behind. I don't, because I have a reason *why* deeply ingrained in my soul: *to accumulate wealth for my children's children*. It is a one-sentence statement. Other side benefits are the cash flow, fun, places to hide bodies. Just kidding—but I do have a story! I had a property, and years before I owned it, the owner had murdered their spouse and then pretended to be a utility company, came, and dug up the body to move it.

Did I mention that there will be hard times? Having a mission will keep you focused and continuously fighting to move forward.

What Is Your Business Model?

Now that you have a mission—a purpose for investing—what is your business model? How will you invest in real estate? Will you buy rentals and/or apartment complexes, or invest in commercial properties?

I won't talk about the pros and cons of each of these; what I am asking you to do is *decide*. Once you choose, stick to that model (most of the time).

You should set criteria for what you are interested in, so that you don't go after all of the "opportunities" that are not opportunities for you. It happens. We decided early on to invest in single-family units, some duplexes in a specific price range, with a certain number of beds and baths. It was our sweet spot, where we could manage and maintain with ease and in very familiar areas. Unfortunately, I got a bit arrogant and thought I could do anything involving real estate. I had a friend who had storage units. He had built a set near the mall, near a few apartment complexes in a modest housing area. Without evaluating the purchase and the storage unit business (which we will talk about later), I told him I would buy them. In a few weeks, they were bought.

In Jim Collins's book *How the Mighty Fall*, he talks about what brings a great company down: *hubris*. Which is Greek for pride. It is something I have battled over and over. Most of the time, I win (see how arrogant that sounds?). This time, I did not.

Storage units are a great business to be in. They are a simple-to-manage arrangement, where people pay you to store their trash because they just can't seem to throw it away. Watch the television show *Storage Wars* on the A&E channel to see what I mean.

When we buy residential real estate, we buy a passive income operation. And, for the most part, it is passive.

When I purchased the storage units, I bought a job. I didn't want another job; I had two already. What I didn't understand about the storage unit business is managing isn't a nine-to-five job—but all day, every day. People will call you while they are standing in front of the units.

It is important to understand that the box you offer these people isn't any different than the next guy's box. In essence, you're selling a box with a lock. If the person answering the phone can't meet the tenant right then, you have lost a sale.

We bought the units at a time when my wife was managing our properties. With kids in tow, she would go to a residential rental property, unlock it, sit in the car with the A/C running, and let the potential tenant browse without her tagging along. It is not the best system, but it was a workable one for her and the kids. If the tenant wanted the house, she would send them to the CPA office to fill out the application, and if approved, call them back to sign the lease within a couple of days.

With storage units, we couldn't do that. There was no application. The potential tenant wanted to fill out the lease agreement right then, put their stuff in, and lock it up. Which means when they call, you need to get over there right then!

The other problem was when the units would get over-locked. At the beginning of the eviction process, typically due to not paying their rent, Angela would put an additional lock on the unit to keep the tenants from getting to their stuff. The tenants would then call my wife and cuss her out. My wife has thick skin, but it happened so often that one day she was so angry she threw the phone across the room. I knew then that we probably needed to hire a property manager.

Unfortunately, the real estate agent/property manager we hired didn't understand storage units either. He thought that if he called the potential tenant back within twenty-four hours, it would be sufficient. No matter how much I tried to explain, he didn't get it or didn't care.

We lost so much money with those units. Whenever some-one called and got the agent's voicemail, they went to the next set of units they could find. I estimate I lost about $12,000 to $20,000 per year on those units because of missed calls.

Later, I bought a smaller set of storage units that was always full, and it helped reduce my losses on the first set. Basically, I broke even each month, until both properties sold together.

The day we sold the storage units was one of the most fan-tastic days ever. It was an expensive lesson, but I did learn that I have a niche, and I need to stick to it.

Your business model should answer the following questions:

1. *What type of investment property works best for us?*
2. *What is the price range that makes sense for us and is within our budget?*
3. *What areas are we most familiar with, and how can we leverage that knowledge?*
4. *How will we evaluate properties in the future?*
5. *What type of property will we say no to?*

If you can easily address these questions with solid answers, you can better develop your overall model. Then you can be-come an expert in that model.

Becoming an expert will lower your frustrations and create momentum with your investment properties. You will be able to move in and out of investments, each time contributing to your profit and net worth.

When we started gaining momentum in the properties, I no longer drove around and looked for properties. It became known in the community that I was a buyer, and people would call me first if they had something to sell. I even bought a few properties sight-unseen based on the recommendation of my wife and our real estate agent. These properties made us money and fit well within our portfolio.

Having a niche in investment property helps you to move faster on properties and evaluate them more effectively. I've had the most trouble when straying outside our business model of single-family residential houses.

Tenants as Customers

An investor with an entrepreneurial mindset sees the tenants as customers. Like any business, you need to know your tenants' likes and dislikes—what is important to them and what is not.

When we began investing, we remodeled every property as if we were going to live there. Our standard was that if we wouldn't live there, we wouldn't rent it. On the surface, that seems reasonable, but it is inward-focused, not customer-focused. We didn't consider what our customers wanted in a rental.

After many years of renting to our niche clientele, we know better what criteria the tenants use to evaluate their properties. We no longer put certain fixtures or door types. For example, the three top needs for people in our niche group are (1) cleanliness, (2) security, and (3) functionality. The custom doors or decorative ceiling fans didn't even enter their thinking. The color on the walls or even central heat and air may not be a factor either.

You need to know your tenants as your customers—and what they are looking for. This will help guide your decisions and drive your revenues. It will make the difference when a tenant is choosing your unit over someone else's.

Thinking of your tenants as customers will also help you remember where the money comes from. Good tenants are hard to find. Great tenants are scarce.

It is important to remember that the tenants are people— people with needs and desires that have good and hard times. They will call the emergency line with either a real issue or a minor maintenance question at the worst possible time.

And despite the upside and positive relationships built when you satisfy a tenant, there are times when those calls are not as easy as fixing a leaky toilet. The longer you're in real estate, the more you will be lied to or called an asshole or threatened with a lawsuit. It isn't personal. There must be a balance struck between *caring for people* and protecting your investment. You must decide where that balance is within the laws of your state.

Processes and Procedures

As an entrepreneur real estate investor, you will need to create *procedures* for the property manager and tenants to follow. This will help keep those boundaries in place between you and your tenants. And *policies* are a safety mechanism to defer to when a tenant asks for something you just can't give.

We will talk more about property management in a later chapter. This discussion is more about why you need these in place.

Procedures are *how you do business*, whereas policies are *the parameters within which you operate*. A procedure dictates when the late notices go out, the eviction suit is initiated, deposits are made—and how you accept payments from tenants. Policies are whether you allow pets, what form of payment you will receive, and when tenants should expect their deposit returned. As with most policies, you will need to know your state, county, and locality laws regarding rental real estate.

When we first began, we went to the local JP—justice of the peace (in Texas, this is a small claims court for eviction suits)—and requested information and procedural instructions for their court. I wish the procedures were all the same in each precinct, but they are not. Also, the laws of the state that they interpret are the same, but the way they interpret them is not.

When my daughter, Kate, started as my property manager at age nineteen, within months, she had her first eviction suit. She went to the JP of the precinct where the house was located, asked for their procedures, and filed the proper paperwork.

I told her, "These suits are usually nothing and the tenants hardly, seldom, show up."

Of course, for her, they did show up...and with their attorney. So, with all the lease documents, deposit history, and other evidence, my daughter showed up to represent our company (as an employee, she could act as an attorney-in-fact). The JP sided with us, and the tenants were ordered to vacate; but for Kate, it is a great story to tell.

Since she came on board, Kate has put a lot of time and effort into creating a policy and procedure manual. You, as an entrepreneur real estate investor, should have something similar. It will make your life easier, and if you must change property managers, you will have something to give them so that they can take over with a minimal learning curve.

Strategic Planning

With real estate, like any business, you need to have a strategy, set goals, and employ tactics that work. In this section, we will only briefly talk about strategic planning for real estate.

We've already discussed why you are beginning this journey. Once you have that purpose in mind, ask yourself, *where do I want to go with this in the future?* This is the goal-setting stage of the planning process. What are your goals for one year, three years, five years, or more?

For us, when we started this adventure, I had a goal of owning one hundred houses. I thought, *man, if I had a hundred houses, that would be awesome!* (I actually said to myself, "awesome.")

I recently ran into a guy that has over three thousand units, houses, apartments, duplexes. I immediately felt like I needed to increase my goal.

Your goals may adapt, but wherever you are now, just put some goals down on paper. Until you write down the goal, it is just a dream.

Also, talk about your goal. Tell people that ask. Let your bankers know, your real estate agent know. The more people you talk to about your goals, the more real it becomes to you.

Your biggest and wildest imagination goal might be thirty properties. That's okay. Everyone's definition of success is different.

I had another goal that tied into the number of properties in our portfolio. It was a net worth or wealth goal. I wanted our net worth to surpass $5 million by the time I was thirty-five.

You may want to add some other quantifiable measurement to track your progress. It is up to you what the finish line might be.

Once I had accumulated one hundred properties, I decided to make a new goal: three hundred houses. I have a ways to go, and now that I met the guy with three thousand units, I will push to see it happen. What comes next is figuring out how to make it happen. What two or three strategies will you employ to see your goals become a reality?

The next chapter talks about finding and evaluating properties. Then there will be a chapter on financing options. Since real estate acquisition includes those two-steps, you might have strategies that include financing, and others where the financing might be just the next step.

When selecting strategies, once again, I recommend sticking to what you know. If you don't know anything, get the education first. I'm not talking about going to school, but reading books, talking to investors, mentors, and your team members.

One strategy may be to gather several investors to buy apartment complexes. This is called *syndication*. Again, we will talk specifics on this later.

Another approach might be to go to the foreclosure auction every month. This strategy requires activities before and after to acquire high-quality properties.

One of my friends from high school, Ron Phillips, wrote a book called *Getting Rich the Right Way*. In it, he describes the specific criteria and strategies he uses for investing in real estate. I like to brainstorm several possible avenues and then choose two or three to put into action.

When we first started out, buying HUD foreclosures was an excellent way to get good properties at low prices. That strategy worked for a while, but later HUD changed the rules and made it a bit harder for investors to have opportunities to bid on properties.

Sometimes the strategies might change. The mission shouldn't change often, if ever. The vision shouldn't change until it's met, unless the environment you operate in changes (note that 2020 did this to many businesses because of COVID-19). The strategies and tactics, however, may change as often as needed to meet the vision.

So now, let's move on to finding excellent properties and evaluating whether they are right for you.

CHAPTER 5

FINDING AND EVALUATING PROPERTY

Finding Property

Where Are They?

What do you do for fun? Do you go on weekend trips to enjoy the city sites with your spouse? Do you have picnics in the park? Or catch a matinée?

My wife and I used to drive around our little town and look for properties! Sounds like a barrel of laughs, right? We would drive slowly in our mini-van—or later in our Suburban—looking for the shiny, red and white "For Sale by Owner" signs that would signal an opportunity (which I will discuss later in this chapter).

Licensed real estate agents started using boxes on their signs that held flyers. It was especially fun to park in front of the house, dash to the sign, and steal a brochure. What a rush! Okay, some of you are obviously not on the same page here, but this was before you could browse or take a virtual tour on the internet. The flyers had pictures and information about the beds, baths, living areas, and square footage. Still not getting excited? I guess you had to be there...and easily entertained.

Up until this point in the book, we haven't even stepped you through buying properties yet. So, let's go get some! Where are they hiding?

Fortunately for you, there are many ways to find properties. The most common is to work with a licensed real estate agent and take advantage of the Multiple Listing Service (MLS) that most licensed real estate agents have access to. There are also foreclosure auctions, tax sale auctions, internet auction services, For Sale By Owners (FSBOs), to name a few. Other ways to find properties are less conventional. They rely on your networking skills and community. This chapter will discuss where to look for suitable properties, and then how to evaluate those properties.

When you look for properties, you are looking for deals. Which means you will need to know the market. When I say *know*, I mean like the "Adam knew his wife, Eve" in the Bible type of know. Pretty damn intimately. A casual knowledge of the market won't give you instincts as to when a house is a steal or not.

You probably think you know the market because you live in it. But when was the last time you bought something there?

Markets change over time, and in some places, they change quickly. You will need to be an astute listener for the ebbs and flows. What about remodeling costs? Have you seen how much lumber costs are now? As I am writing this, there is a lumber shortage in Texas. The cost of a two-by-four is three times what it was just last year. How does that affect what you are willing to pay for a house in need of some tender loving care? Remember, when you buy a property, your profit becomes constrained by that cost. We will talk about evaluating property later, but before we even begin looking, do your homework. You know this; you are an entrepreneur!

Working with a Real Estate Agent

Most people, when looking for property, use a real estate agent. They offer a great place to start. As one of your team members, your real estate agent will be one of the best sources of property leads available. As we discussed in chapter three, finding the right real estate agent will help you find the right properties.

Starting out, the quantity of offers made on existing homes for sale will increase the chances of closing on one or more. My wife loves to search realtor.com or loopnet.com for property. Even if we aren't in a buying mode, she is scouring the internet for good deals. It keeps her informed of the changes in the market, and she loves looking at houses.

Before the internet, the only way to look at houses' interiors was to make appointments with real estate agents. Just a hint: they don't like that. They will be polite and professional, but if you are doing this and have no plans to buy, you are stealing from them. You are stealing their time, which is precious.

When working with a real estate agent, you must first sit down and go over the type of house you're looking for. Don't be too specific, as your perfect house is probably not out there. This isn't like looking for a personal residence where you have clear "must-haves." It is more of a range within which you would be interested in looking. It may take several meetings or showings for the real estate agent to get to know you and your preferences.

Knowing the market like you do—and how much the remodel will cost in general terms—will help you make a buying decision. You may be looking for "turn-key" rentals. Houses that do not need any remodel are clean and immediately desirable to potential tenants. Or you may be looking for diamonds in the rough. When we started, we would find the properties no one wanted in good neighborhoods. With a short, two-to-three-week remodel period and remodel budget, we could put the house on the market before the first payment or quickly after.

As a strategy, finding turn-key properties is a good one, but you will usually need to put down more cash and must spend a little more. Honestly, finding turn-key properties is my preference. I hate having to do work on a house before putting it up for rent. But my strategy has changed depending on our ability to find laborers and costs of materials.

Be sure to let your real estate agent know if your strategy is changing or making a temporary turn. Your real estate agent can be such a great partner in finding properties and building your inventory. Be sure to thank them for their efforts, and even if they haven't sent you anything to look at in a while or you haven't bought anything in a while, send them a gift to let them know you value them.

For Sale by Owner (FSBOs)

For Sale by Owner signs jump out at me like no other sign! Something on the inside of me gets a little giddy when I see one.

I need to tell you something about me. It is personal. I love to buy things. Really. It is a bit of an adrenaline addiction. My family knows this. Now you know. In addition to buying houses, I like to buy cars. Also, I like to buy trucks and motorcycles. At one time, I had three motorcycles. I won't tell you how that came to be, but it shouldn't have happened.

FSBO houses may be a good deal, or they may not be. Investors like them because there usually aren't any real estate agent fees included in the closing. That doesn't mean that you aren't paying "retail." The owner wants to keep what they would otherwise have paid the agent.

I like FSBO houses because they offer a direct negotiation with the seller. As we will discuss in a later chapter on negotiation, dealing directly with the decision-maker makes the negotiation faster and usually puts it in your favor. The truth is that the seller probably doesn't do many real estate deals during the year (unless they are an investor like you). That inexperience may work to your advantage.

Usually, FSBOs are poorly marketed, so they may not have very many competing offers. It sounds like I am playing up using a real estate agent for selling houses. Truthfully, for our flips or my personal residences, I would not even consider selling on my own. The value of an excellent real estate agent cannot be understated in these scenarios. But if you are seller-financing your houses, yes, of course, use that glorious red and white "For Sale by Owner" sign!

Even if I am not looking to buy, if I see an FSBO sign in a yard, I will likely take a picture of the sign and call when I get home or back to the office. I can't help myself. When my wife and I would drive around looking for houses, the FSBOs were my favorites.

Networking Contacts

After you've bought houses for a while, people will come out of the woodwork to see if you want to buy their homes. You don't have to wait to get these leads from strangers and friends. You can be proactive.

There is an organization famous for posting ads with a phrase that they somehow trademarked. It is similar to "I acquire unlovely residences"; by the way, I'm trademarking that phrase! From this, they receive lots of leads on crappy houses that they try to make beautiful.

You can do some of this by creating an email list of potential sellers and investors who might have excess inventory. Or find houses in your market that are vacant and in need of some love, and contact the owners directly. *How*, you ask? Good old-fashioned snail mail. A handwritten letter goes a long way to connecting with people on a personal level. You can usually find the owner's mailing address on the county appraisal district website, or your state's equivalent if the homeowner doesn't reside there. With social media today, you can also message your friends and family that you are buying houses, asking them to contact you if they hear of anything coming available. You will need to supply them with some criteria, but this grassroots effort will help get the word out. You might even sweeten the deal with a finder's fee if you buy a house that was referred. It doesn't have to be much, but those who refer properties to you will remember the consideration on your part.

As a CPA, some of my clients have been good sources of properties. Once I let them know that I was buying, a few reached out to tell me about their houses or houses from other friends and family. It is amazing what you can find just from word of mouth.

I would try to let many of your friend groups know that you are buying. If you don't have many friend groups or friends with real estate, there are business networking groups that you can join. Those groups might be the Lions Club, Rotary, BNI International, Toastmasters, political party groups, etc. Whatever group that you join, you should be there out of sincerity and not just to gain. You should believe in the mission and purpose of the group. That is how good friends are made, and trust is established. In the natural course of relating to the group, they will find out you are a real estate investor and will keep an eye out for you.

The same can be said about affinity groups you might join. I love martial arts and have been a part of Tae Kwon Do schools off and on since I was fifteen. These schools tend to be close-knit and are a terrific source for potential real estate deals. Again, the idea is not to join a class to gain new properties, but because you want to be there for the martial arts (or whatever activity you join).

When getting leads or referrals from friends for their houses or properties they know about, it is important to remind them that you are an investor. Investors don't usually pay the retail or market rates for the property. Since the maximum amount of money we can make on a property is set when we purchase, finding deals is the goal of most investors.

I've had several friends call and say that they are moving out of town and need to sell their homes fast. We usually talk for a while about what they are looking for and the condition of the home. I let them know I will offer them 15 to 25 percent less than if they listed the property with a real estate agent. I am very up front about that. I don't want them to hear from their neighbor that they sold their house with "so-and-so" real estate agent and got $30,000 more than what I paid. The neighbor won't tell them they had to spend $10,000 to $15,000 to remodel or upgrade the kitchen or that it took six months to find a buyer. If you consider all those things plus the agent's fees, my offer would only be 5 percent less than what they could have netted. They may not make the same calculation in their heads. It is better to just tell them, "If you want to close quickly, avoid real estate agent's fees, and remodel costs, we would be happy to give you an offer below market—but still a good offer."

Auctions

One well-known source of properties is the *real estate auction*. There are several types of auctions available today. The *foreclosure auction* in Texas happens on the first Tuesday of every month, usually on the courthouse steps or some other designated area on county property. Auctions may be run by an auctioneer, depending on the sellers and how many properties they have to auction. The sellers are the banks (or holders of the real estate lien note) that foreclosed on the homes from mortgagees.

Some people see this as a cruel practice, but it isn't. Most mortgages are non-recourse, meaning that once the bank, financial institution, or holder of the note (holder) takes possession of the property, the debt is fully satisfied. It may hurt their credit, but the bank cannot take anything else from them. The holder then, by law, must auction the property with a beginning bid of the loan balance plus any legal fees. This gives the former homeowner one more chance to get the house back. The only caveat is that the amount is due in full by the end of the auction day. If the holder wants to, they can bid on the property and usually do with a starting bid.

If you're going to go to the auction, you should first get the list of properties up for auction, called trustee sales, and do a drive-by to see what condition they are in. If the previous owners are still in the property, which may be the case, you can only take a street view.

Some buyers try to meet with the mortgagees to buy the house directly from them before the auction. This isn't a bad strategy, but it takes time and a considerable amount of boldness. Borrowers who have gotten to this stage have until the auction begins to "cure" with the holder, which means to pay any amounts in arrears plus late fees and attorney's fees. This is a strategy to buy and get the seller to finance the property to you, the investor. I will talk a bit more about seller financing later.

If the previous owners are no longer in the property, you might be able to look in the windows, but more often than not, you can't go in. Before you bid, you should check to see if there are any tax liens or vendors' liens on the property. Those will have to be paid before you get a clear title. You will need to learn to do some title research to do this well and avoid surprises.

You can hire your attorney to help research this for you. Most of the time, a paralegal will be sent to the county clerk's office, or if the county is in the twenty-first century, everything will be available online. You may wish to pay the paralegal to do the research once or twice and have them show you how they prepare the search. This may give you the confidence to do this part yourself, or reinforce your great decision to have them handle this part.

The foreclosure auction is just one of the auctions available today. A new method of selling property has been created for bold sellers: *the internet auction.* These properties are not necessarily foreclosures or distressed properties. You can find some on eBay or other real-estate-specific sites that offer a more convenient way to bid on properties than the standard real estate contract method. The offer usually contains the same language and an escrow deposit with the bid, but it bypasses the haggling. You submit an offer, and within minutes or a few days, you are notified if you are the winning bid. Depending on the auction, you may need to provide funds immediately, or have forty-five days to close the deal. I don't hate this method of buying, but it comes with a lot of risks.

The last auction we will discuss is the *tax sale auction.* These properties have been foreclosed on by the county, or local taxing authority, for non-payment of real estate taxes, sometimes called "ad valorem" taxes. The bidding usually starts at the amount the taxpayer/owner owed and goes up from there. It can be the most inexpensive way to acquire property, but there is plenty of competition at the auctions, which can drive up your cost. Also, there is the risk that the previous owner can come back within a certain period of time and reclaim the property. In Texas, the previous owner has up to 180 days to reclaim the property by paying you what you paid for the property, plus costs to repair, insure, and some other nominal expenses, plus a markup. The risk is that you won't get a clear title until after 180 days. This restricts your ability to finance the property, and any remodel plans.

Be careful to get an understanding of the tax sale/sheriff's sale properties in your state before you make your bid. I am not an attorney, and there may be things here I am leaving out. I just mention this type of auction, because I have clients who have created a good portfolio from these tax sale auctions.

Other Investors

Another valuable source of potential properties is other investors. Where to find them? We just talked about the best place to find them: the bank foreclosure auctions will bring out many of the local players in your area. Often, they have more opportunities come their way than they can handle, so they look to other investors to spread the wealth. If you get to know a few, you may have some success buying wholesale from them. They will make a profit from you, but it may still be in your profit zone as well.

Early in our real estate journey, we had met several local investors. After visiting with one for a while, I asked if he had some properties he would sell. He said he would get back to me. After a few weeks, he gave me a list of nine properties. We drove by and looked inside the ones that we could, and after a few weeks, they belonged to us.

Another time I was at church when I ran into a lady to whom I had sold fourteen properties a few years before. I asked how she was doing and how the properties were. She said not well. Her son, who managed them for her, was about to leave for New Jersey to go to school. She would have no one to manage them. I asked her to consider selling them back to me, but at a discount. She said she would. We bought back the fourteen we had sold her plus two others that she had purchased from other investors. I was happy to have more potential income, and she was glad not to manage them.

Evaluating Property

Set Criteria

Before you buy—before you draw up a contract, before you even think about going to look for property—you need to set the criteria of what a suitable property looks like to you. The requirements may be a minimum number of bedrooms or bathrooms, minimum square footage, and/or price points that you will not go over. Your criteria can change over time, but for the most part, they should guide you and the partners who are working with you in finding properties.

Whatever standards you set, you should see them as guidelines more than hard and fast rules. When you start out, I caution you to stay within the guidelines. This will keep you investing in familiar properties. You will develop somewhat of a niche in your property choices. Later on, you may have opportunities to purchase properties outside your boundaries, but then you will know the challenges that may occur when you do. When we bought the storage units, it was vastly outside our regular purchase history. We should never have even considered it. I am not saying storage units are not a good investment. For some people, they are right within their wheelhouse. But for us, we did not understand the property type enough before we purchased them to know how to manage them well. If we had taken some time to research and talk to others in storage units who do well at them, we could have been prepared and made the necessary adjustments to our business model. But we didn't. And they didn't fit with our passive income generation model.

On the other hand, we have purchased larger homes with lower margins and higher maintenance costs and have been successful. The variance from our model was not enough to disrupt our lives. We had done enough research and understood the market sufficiently to do well in those higher-end homes.

When we started, our primary market was two-to-three-bedroom homes with one or more bathrooms from 700 to 1,800 square feet. These homes were in lower-middle-class areas and stayed occupied very well.

When times are good, people move out of apartments and into my houses. When times are bad, people move out of the larger square footage homes into my houses. It's my safe zone for investment property. Two people working full-time at just a bit better than minimum wage could afford my houses.

That is where we began investing. As I said, sometimes the criteria can move, or you might make one or two purchases outside your usual investment niche. We began buying larger three-bedroom, two-bath houses around 2,000 to 2,500 square feet and experienced good results. We didn't get rid of the other homes; we just started buying more middle-class homes. It helped that our cash flow and income from our day jobs is more than when we started and gives us more capital to work with.

Once you have your criteria set—based on your capital, knowledge of the market, and business model—you can move forward finding those properties. We will talk about the financing and closing process later, but let's assume that you just closed on your first house. Now what?

Set Remodel Budget

When evaluating a property, before you buy, you should have a remodel budget. Even though the last section ended with you closing on your first house, you should have prepared a rough budget for remodeling before you ever made a bid on the property. A rough budget should be completed with a contractor or yourself. After a while, you will know the costs of labor and materials for certain jobs. There are tools that you can use to help. If you search the internet for remodel cost estimators, you may find some handy tools that use your zip code to figure the costs depending on what type of room, size of the room, and what is being done.

When I started, because I am an accountant nerd, I used an Excel spreadsheet to estimate costs based on the jobs needed. Without getting into the weeds of creating your own spreadsheet, I would recommend looking into the cost of builder materials and labor costs for your area. You might ask around at what people paid for replacing a heating and air conditioning unit (HVAC), for example. Without calling around and asking for specific bids, this may be time-consuming, but it is better than being surprised after the fact.

If you are a handy person yourself, you might decide to do most of the labor yourself. I would still compute the cost of labor into your estimate. You don't get to deduct your labor or use it to offset gain when the property is sold, but it is a good idea to know what it would have cost. With this information, you can decide if your time is worth putting into the remodel.

As a real estate entrepreneur, you will probably lean towards doing it yourself. I did in the beginning—until my day job earned more than the labor costs, and time with my family became more valuable to me. In the early days, working on properties was synonymous with time with the family. My wife, kids, mother-in-law, and father-in-law were all there with us.

My father-in-law, Larry, took a week's vacation to work on our first home with us. Later in life, after a few kids were thrown into the mix, I decided to replace the carpet in our new house. Larry again took some time off to help me. We only needed to pull up the old carpet, clean the cement floor, put down the new pad, and install the carpet. Easy enough, right?

On the way to the ER, I used language that shouldn't be said to the father of your wife and "Papa" to your children. During the simple installation, I had a carpet knife accident. Anyone who has used carpet utility knives knows that they cut carpet like a hot knife through butter. You can imagine what they can do to the flimsy material surrounding our muscles and organs called skin.

I opened the skin to the bone on my left index knuckle. Knowing that I would pass out at any moment—I have this reaction to blood sometimes (especially my own blood)—I yelled at my father-in-law about what direction he was taking to get to the hospital. I tried to let him know I could lose consciousness, take my hand off the wound, and bleed out in his truck. During the ride to the hospital, I dreaded that he might have to carry me into the ER.

Thankfully, the adrenaline from the yelling kept me conscious long enough to tell the nurse my name before I sank to the floor. Since then, I don't do any work myself. I let the professionals handle it.

A rough budget should be calculated by room, plus any exterior costs, HVAC, plumbing, or electric needs. Once you buy the house, you'll probably need to get bids to achieve a more solid number. For now, you're just setting a budget to determine if the property you are bidding on will make you money after deducting the expected costs.

In your rough budget, you should add some costs for what you don't know or can't see. In remodeling, there is almost always something in that category. Start with 10 percent of identified costs as your buffer.

Rent Income Targets

Part of the property evaluation should always include your *rent income target*. This amount is the range between the maximum and minimum expected rents for the subject property. It's important that you can "make your margins" at the minimum expected rent income level. *Margin* is the difference between rental income and mortgage payments, property taxes, insurance, and management fees.

To get an idea of potential rents—and thus determine rental income—research local advertisers like the newspaper,

Craigslist, and Facebook Marketplace. Also, if you have a good relationship with a real estate agent, they can look up local rents on MLS. In addition, most cities have a housing and urban development department (HUD). Not to be confused with the federal version, these local departments help distribute state and federal housing benefits to qualified candidates. They usually have a listing of maximum approved rents. The list is generally in a table that has tiers by the number of bedrooms and bathrooms. It may also have "all-bills-paid" versus "rent-only" listings. These lists don't limit what you can charge for rent, but they do limit the amount the government entity will subsidize. Some potential tenants qualify for full subsidies, meaning they get the maximum benefit, while others only get a part of the subsidy. For those who only receive a portion, they must come up with the rest of the rent. Most landlords will set their rents at the top of the tier for the number of bedrooms and baths they have available. If you want to market your property to these tenants, you just need to call the local HUD office and tell them what you have available. There are specific basic criteria your property must have to ensure the tenant's health, safety, and security, but it isn't usually that difficult to pass their inspection.

I have a spreadsheet to determine the gross margin (rent less mortgage payments) and net margin (rent less mortgage payments, taxes, insurance, management fees, utilities, and a repair allowance). Knowing the rent targets for the property beforehand will help you determine the cash flow.

Most of the time, a property should be evaluated by itself. Each property should contribute to the margin of your real estate business empire. Much like a product, each property must justify its inclusion in your inventory. Having said that, there are times that I will evaluate a group of properties together. Usually, it's because we are buying more than one property from a single seller. Like when purchasing an apartment complex, the sum of the units should be evaluated together. Why is that? As stated, when I consider a property, I include the mortgage payment. This is so that I don't overextend myself but instead ensure I have more than enough to cover my debt service. Eventually, though, the properties will be paid off.

When buying in a group, sometimes you can refinance or get your bank to release property from the combined lien when the loan on the properties is less than 50 to 60 percent of the fair market value of the properties. This could turn a low-margin house into a high-margin house by refinancing the remaining properties themselves or paying off the loan altogether.

Knowing your market and setting the rental income targets before buying will help you keep adding cash flow instead of just adding debt.

Appraisals and Comparable Sales

Before putting an offer on a house, you should know something about the market. I'm sure I've written that before. You should know what other houses in the area have sold for and how they compare to the property you are buying. You can usually get this information from a real estate agent or from realtor.com. The latter doesn't always have the latest or most accurate information. A real estate agent is your best source.

When comparing houses, it is not always an apples-to-apples comparison. You can't just say this 3/2 (three bedroom, two bath) sold for $230,000, so this 3/2 should sell for the same amount. You must adjust for the differences in quality (remodeled and updated versus not), size of rooms, location, overall square footage, central heat and air, etc. In certain areas, the schools in the area can drive up the demand for the region and therefore drive up the price. Two identical homes in different areas of the same town can have very different prices.

It is essential to know how the appraisals of homes are calculated when making offers, so that you aren't surprised at closing. Both the seller and the buyer can be surprised. I was selling a commercial building that had several office spaces and was in a great location. The list price was $130,000, but the appraisal came back well under the list price.

Unfortunately, new regulations (the hated Dodd-Frank Act) made it impossible for the buyer or the seller to choose which appraiser they would like to use. Even though the buyer pays for the appraisal, they now have no say in who does the appraisal. Also, once an appraisal is reported to the lender at less than the sale price, there isn't much the seller can do. You can pay for another appraisal by another random company, yet the lender does not have to consider it. In addition, appraisers get a little chippy when you call and want to provide information regarding the property's value.

I don't support trying to influence an appraiser's opinion; however, if I have information not available to the public that could impact the property's value, I will submit that to the appraiser. The appraisers I've dealt with were not open to receiving that information, but I've still tried. Some are, and you should remember those who are willing to get the numbers right no matter where they get the information.

Now that you've evaluated the property and are ready to purchase, we'll explore some financing options available to entrepreneur real estate investors.

CHAPTER 6

FINANCING PROPERTY ACQUISITION

Financing Introduction

When I was in my junior year of high school, I watched this girl walk into the school. My locker was by the entrance, so I was perfectly positioned to see who was coming in. I told my friend Jeremy, whose locker was next to mine, "I'm going to be with her!" I may have added some profanities back then, but this is a family book.

Immediately, I planned how I would win her affection. First, I approached her and asked for her name and where she was from. It was a small school, so new people stuck out immediately. She said her name was Amy and they had come from Miami. Her dad was in the military, so they moved a lot.

Over the next few days and weeks, she got to know me, and I got to know her. When I found out she didn't have a car and rode the bus, I spent more time with her in the morning and afternoon. By chance, she lived around the corner from us, and I could swing by to pick her up on my way to school.

We ended up dating for over six months. In high school, that's a long time. I eventually screwed things up with her, but I learned about myself—and my weaknesses. That discussion isn't for this book.

Finding a lender is a lot like dating. You need to get to know each lender's loan programs and hopefully their loan officers as well. It can sometimes feel like you are totally exposing yourself financially. There will be a full disclosure of your financial position, but the lender is your partner.

Financing can be the most stressful and challenging part of the real estate entrepreneur's journey, especially if you are just starting out and don't have a credit history or, worse, have bad credit. These factors shouldn't deter you from beginning your real estate journey. You just need to know how the game is played, its rules, and what makes lenders want to partner with you.

In this chapter, we will go over the various ways you can finance property. There are several, each with its pros and cons. I have used most of them to get into properties where other options weren't available.

The key here is to *never give up*. Just because a bank or mortgage company denies you doesn't mean your journey is over. In fact, sometimes, that is a blessing in disguise, just like when you ask out a girl (or guy) who isn't right for you. When they say no, you should be thankful.

Be creative about your financing. As you learn the various options, you'll see that financing real estate isn't as stressful anymore—that in fact, many lenders will work *with* you. Once you have a good portfolio, some lenders will bend over backward to have your business. And you should always be grateful and gracious with them.

It must be a two-way street; both sides should be bringing things to the table. You get your knowledge of real estate and management skills; they bring their cash and advice. It is a symbiotic relationship, like a good marriage. However, if you get overextended or manage the properties poorly, the lender can become a cruel taskmaster.

Financing is leverage. It is the power of other people's money to create wealth and cash flow. You could save up to buy a house in cash, or use a lender and speed up the process. Dave Ramsey, author of *Total Money Makeover*, is adamantly against debt. And rightly so, for a person who overextended himself so much that he went into bankruptcy.

Debt financing can be a wealth-building tool. But like many tools, it can become a deadly weapon. Changes in the interest rates by the Fed, demand for housing, shifts in your market, or large employers laying off people in large numbers in small markets can all affect your ability to remain profitable and pay your debt service. We will talk about two essential variables in the "Managing Real Property" chapter: your *loan-to-value ratio* and your *cash flow margin*.

If the loan against the property is over 80 percent of its value, you are in dangerous territory. A slight dip in the market or change in interest rates can reduce the value of your property. This doesn't have immediate consequences, but for resale or refinancing, it could be detrimental.

Your cash flow margin is the difference between your rental income and debt service. I usually like that ratio to be two-to-one or a 50 percent margin, where rental income is two times the debt service. Lenders call this the debt service coverage rate (DSCR). I prefer to use the cash flow margin when assessing my profitability, since my focus is cash flow.

A 50 percent margin rate doesn't always happen, though. While some deviation from this number is okay, if you are running at a 25 percent margin, you won't have enough left over after the debt service to maintain the property. You may be barely covering the real estate taxes and hazard insurance.

So, let's get into the various ways to finance your property and give you tools to use in building your real estate empire.

Conventional Financing

If you are not familiar with the vocabulary of financing, you should probably take a short course on loans, compound interest, amortization, and the like. There are hundreds of videos on YouTube to get acquainted with the terminology. Having said that, let's look at *conventional financing*.

Conventional financing is any financing that doesn't fall into one of the multiple special programs, like FHA or VA loans. It usually requires a 20 percent down payment, but not always.

Low down or *zero down* financing isn't as available now as in my early days of investing. It still exists with some banks and credit unions. The down payment for investment property, depending on the institution, can be as little as 0 to 5 percent.

When I started, I called almost every bank in town to ask them about their investment property loan programs. Some bankers were hesitant to speak with me. Since the terms you receive depend on your credit score and the strength of your balance sheet, I had to ask them what their best terms were, just so I could compare them.

Note, you should shop around before you need the bank. If you're shopping while there is a contract in hand, you may make a hasty decision about your lender. Hasty decisions are usually the wrong decisions.

As I stated before, the interest rate and terms aren't your only consideration when choosing a lender. Some banks are easier to work with than others. Also, the closer you are to talking with a decision-maker, the better. Larger banks have more layers between the loan officer and those making the underwriting decisions.

For an investment property, the rules are much different than for a homestead, a personal residence. It is generally easier and much less paperwork to get an investment property loan than an owner-occupied home mortgage. Most states have laws that protect a person's personal residence. That makes getting a mortgage a bit more cumbersome. Terms for conventional financing can be for fifteen, twenty, twenty-five, or thirty years. With most commercial banks, you can get a fixed rate for the term. Some smaller banks, however, will only lock in the interest rate for one to five years. Even though the amortization period may be twenty years, in one to five years, you will have to renew the loan for another one to five years. These are called ARMs or *adjustable-rate mortgages*. The interest rates adjust automatically at each renewal period based on a predetermined formula. That formula is usually tied to the prime rate as published in *The Wall Street Journal* every Thursday. For example, the prime rate may be 3 percent, and the ARM mortgage states that the rate will adjust at prime plus 2 percentage points, or 5 percent. The longer the fixed period, the better. The key is to get the shortest term possible while still achieving your target cash flow margin.

Conventional financing is the ideal method of financing of all the techniques discussed later. The more properties you have in your portfolio, the easier it will be to get conventional financing. Each new income producing property adds to your reportable income. Also, the more properties you have, the lower the bank considers their risk.

A form of conventional financing is a *construction loan*. This may sound like you're building a complete house, but that isn't the only use for this type of loan. I've purchased houses with zero upfront cash, because I effectively showed the bank the list of planned improvements. In some cases, the amount of work would exceed 20 percent of the sale price or appraised value, and I was given money at closing to get the project started. This hardly denotes a zero-down purchase, since you have to pay for the work being done; but it does let you spread the down payment over a few months while the project is being worked on.

Some banks allow you to pay interest only on the notes for a set period, like six months. After six months, the note is converted to a conventional loan and amortized. The goal is to have the remodel finished and rented before the end of the interest-only period. Depending on the extent of the remodel, it may be less than the interest-only period.

There are times, because of unforeseen circumstances, the remodel takes longer. That shouldn't discourage you. If you budget the interest payments for the entire six months into your costs, and maybe one or two months of the amortized payments, you will have enough buffer for a longer remodel job. Also, sometimes banks will allow you to extend the interest only period.

Seller as the Lender

Seller-financed properties are just that; the seller becomes the lender. Not all sellers are open to this kind of deal. With smaller deals, particularly single-family residences, you may find a seller here and there who is willing to finance the property. Though it may cost you higher interest rates, you might get by with little or no down payment.

We bought one of our personal residences like this. The sellers were asking $120,000 for an over 3,000-square-foot house in West Texas. I asked them to seller-finance it for a short time period. Then when I had more capital, we refinanced it with a bank. I call this the *seller-financed two-step*.

Many investors buy property, do some work to improve it, sell the property on a seller-financed note. You may be able to get a deal from these investors, but it is not likely. Usually, they are selling at the top of the market. I only do the seller-financed two-step if the property will appraise for much more than the purchase price.

To refinance, you must be at or below 80 percent of the appraised value. Otherwise, you will need to provide the additional cash or continue paying the higher interest rates.

With the lottery winner I mentioned, I bought sixteen properties from her, only paying closing costs. Since the period on the balloon note was five years, I refinanced without any trouble. The market values of the properties had modest growth, and we had significantly raised the rents, making them more profitable.

These types of transactions don't come without risks. With a balloon note, the seller is under no obligation to modify or renew the loan for another five years. If I wasn't able to refinance, the seller could have taken all of the properties back.

Hard-Money Lenders

Hard-money lenders are individuals or small business entities that lend at higher than usual interest rates to people they know, with special terms that differ from most conventional loans.

"Wait," you say, "are you talking about loan sharks?" No. Although the interest rates may be higher than other financial institutions, hard-money lenders take collateral with the loan, so there is no need to break any legs.

Usually, a hard-money lender is someone you know. They have excess cash and are willing to lend on short-term loans with high interest rates.

There are also some hard-money lending institutions. A quick Google search, and you can find several in your area and a few national organizations.

I haven't personally used a hard-money lender, but those I know who have applied this option only used people they knew and trusted.

The key with a hard-money loan is the term. You don't want to have a 9 percent loan for more than a few months. Find another conventional lender to refinance the deal as soon as you close, maybe after finishing some remodeling to increase the appraisal.

You may be tempted after refinancing to keep the loan outstanding. I wouldn't recommend this. Each time you pay off the hard-money lender, they gain confidence in your business model. Some in my hometown have built up an extensive portfolio of houses using the same hard-money lender.

The ones you find online work more like a lending institution, except most don't lend based on your credit. They only look at the value of the property. The benefit here is that if they lend at 70 to 75 percent of the property's *after remodel value* (ARV), and the property sale price is 60 percent of ARV, this becomes a no-money-down purchase. Qualifying takes a much shorter time, and funding can be done within ten days. The downside is that if you haven't refinanced it before the end of the term, they are happy to add that property to their portfolio.

Line of Credit

Using a *line of credit* (LOC) to help finance property can be an excellent way to buy property—or fund the down payment for property. Lines of credit are sometimes collateralized and work more like a signature loan.

A few banks that I work with offer a small line of credit when you create a business checking account. Those LOCs are helpful for funding remodels or down payments on smaller houses, but not necessarily buying a house outright. It is a higher interest revolving credit loan that is meant to meet short-term cash flow needs.

Another type of LOC is those collateralized with a certificate of deposit (CD), securities in a brokerage account, or another piece of property free of a mortgage, liens, or encumbrances.

When you collateralize property, you still enjoy the benefits of ownership—like rent, interest, or dividends—so this type of financing is very attractive to those with significant assets. Margin accounts with your securities brokerage accounts can be used as a line of credit as well. As long as you have met the margin requirements, you can borrow against your securities to purchase real estate, buy a car, or go on vacation. I am not recommending any of those actions, but if you have securities and want to get started in real estate, this might be an option for you.

Syndication

This part sounds like organized crime—a group of underhanded gangsters forming an organization to take over the city. I have always loved mob movies and true-crime documentaries about their lives. But no, that is not what *syndication* is. It instead involves organizing a group of investors to purchase a large package of homes or a few multi-family apartment complexes.

It sounds more complicated than it is. Using a limited partnership, which we will discuss in the next chapter, the general partner is the manager of the syndicate. That person or entity finds other investors willing to invest in the project with an expected rate of return for the first few years as limited partners. You can also use a limited liability company (LLC) if the entity is managed by the managers instead of the members. If the project is successful, the general partner will sometimes offer to buy out the limited partners' interest by refinancing the property. So that you don't break any securities laws, your investors must be accredited investors and file Form D with the Securities Exchange Commission (SEC). Please review

Rule 506 of Regulation D as explained at www.investor.gov. This site is hosted by the SEC. An alternative to filing Form D and using accredited investors is a form of syndication that is more like a joint venture than selling interests in a limited partnership or LLC.

I once attempted to buy an apartment complex this way. I was pretty young and didn't have a lot of cash for the down payment. I went to a few individuals—clients, who I thought would easily have the cash between them to help me manage the investment and credit to purchase the property. It turned out that neither of them had any cash to put down. I had one-third of the down payment money and just needed the other two-thirds. The deal fell through, and I lost the contract.

The point here is if you are going to use syndication or joint ventures, or find other investors to help with financing in full or the down payment, you need to vet them first. One way to do this is by creating an application to join the investor group. If I had done just a bit of due diligence beforehand, I would have been able to find investors who could have executed that deal.

Refinancing

One thing that will help you finance real estate is understanding the difference between purchase money financing and *refinancing*.

For most bank loan programs, a conventional loan for investment property will be 80 percent of the sale price or appraisal, whichever is lower. That means that you will have to come up with at least 20 percent down.

In some cases, when the appraisal is less than the sale price, you may have to bring even more cash to closing than just 20 percent plus closing costs. When you refinance a property, most bank programs will loan at 80 percent of appraised value.

Earlier I shared about the seller-finance/refinance two-step to purchasing houses. This is why it works. When you are the recorded owner of a property, what you paid for the property is no longer relevant. What matters is what it will appraise for. After some experience in your market, you will gain a general idea of the appraised value.

We have been right about the value of a property a large percentage of the time, but occasionally we get it wrong. Sometimes it is because of the property characteristics, location, or age; sometimes, the appraiser is super conservative.

Appraisers can sometimes get sued. That makes them hesitant to use comparable sales that aren't "exactly" comparable.

Once, I put a contract on a house that I knew was worth 20 percent more than the contract price. The appraisal came back so low that I had to walk away from the deal. What was the justification? I suspect that the house was too close to commercial businesses to be appraised as a single-family home. We could have paid another appraiser and possibly gotten a more realistic number, but I wasn't that excited about the house anyway, so I let it go.

Before the Dodd-Frank Act, I would have added an appraiser as one of your team members. Not one that you had influence over, but one whose appraisals you trusted. Now, appraisers are selected randomly by the bank on a rotation.

When refinancing an investment property, the appraisal is critical. If you don't like the number you are getting from the appraiser, wait thirty days and try again with a different appraiser. You are allowed to request a different appraiser than the first time.

Sometimes, you also might be able to submit, through the bank, information about non-listed sales that the appraiser may not know about. These comparable sales may help the appraiser understand the off-market value and get closer to what you believe the market value actually is. You shouldn't, however, try to influence an appraiser to "get to" your number. Submitting new information isn't influence. The appraiser can decide to ignore the new information or use it. That is what they are supposed to do.

Ultimately the appraisal will protect both the buyer and the lender from making a bad investment. It is a subjective line of work, but it is meant to be another layer of protection in the industry.

There are times to refinance and times not to refinance. Some investors live their lives on the edge of the loan-to-value line. They refinance to pull the "tax-free" cash from appreciation out of their properties. I don't recommend that practice. You should only refinance for a few reasons.

One is what we just discussed: the seller-finance/refinance two-step.

Another is to recuperate any cash outlay from a significant remodel. Usually, I try to pay for these out of operating income, but sometimes it is best to refinance to conserve cash.

The other reason might be to purchase another property. If you have a property with significant equity and can refinance and stay well under 70 percent of loan to value, I'd consider using that equity to make that purchase.

Foreclosures and Short Selling

HUD/VA Foreclosures

When we started, we loved buying foreclosures. Usually, we bought *HUD, VA,* or other *government foreclosures*. These were generally listed on a website run by the government, and we had to use a real estate agent to place our bid on the website.

For the first few weeks of the bid, the auction was only open to "owner-occupants." This meant that the buyer would have to live in that house for twelve months following the purchase. Several unscrupulous investors in town would bid under other family members' names or ignore the restriction altogether. There wasn't much enforcement in the process. We followed the rules and still scored some quality homes for less than retail, wholesale prices.

Unfortunately, the government changed the way they marketed these houses. They used to set the price based on the amount they needed to recover from the loan that was in default. This method had little to do with the actual market value of the home. An investor's paradise, it was! But then those running the government programs realized that they could get more for those houses than what they had in them, so they set up a system with local real estate agents. Local agents who knew the market would set the starting bid price. If no one bid, or the bid was less than what the government had set as their minimum, the price might be lowered. Each Thursday was the final bid day, so the price would be reduced again if the property were still available on Friday.

These are still great places to find properties, although in certain markets, there may not be many foreclosures available. For available HUD homes, visit www.hudhomestore.com. The website www.vrmproperties.com also has links to the VA homes for sale from the Veterans Affairs department. You don't have to be a veteran to purchase; however, veterans do get preferential treatment.

Bank Foreclosures

You can also find foreclosed properties with your standard *bank foreclosures*. These properties are usually auctioned off once per month.

In Texas, the auctions are on the first Tuesday of every month. The county clerk generally designates where the auctions are held, either at the county courthouse or somewhere on county property.

When a bank forecloses on a property, they usually appoint a substitute trustee to handle the auction. These auctions are sometimes called "trustee sales."

In some counties, an auctioneer is hired to conduct the auction, while in smaller counties or counties with fewer properties to sell, the trustee manages the auction themselves.

The downside of this auction is that you must have the funds to execute the trustee's deed that day, usually by 5:00 p.m. Each trustee decides how the funds can be received: by wire, business check, or cashier's check.

One thing to remember about auctions: if you win the auction, you might be the sucker who paid too much! It seems that every auction has some emotional connection between the buyer and the item. The bid winner may have gotten excited during the auction process and paid more than they had planned. See the TV show *Storage Wars* for examples of this phenomenon.

In any auction, the wise investor will have done their research and determined their starting and maximum bid. If the auction goes above that maximum bid, the investor should walk away.

Short Sales

Short sales are closely connected to foreclosures. The key here is to find a house that is in foreclosure and offer the lender an amount that will satisfy the debt and release the house from foreclosure. To do this, you must communicate with the current borrowers and work out a solution for them that is advantageous for everyone.

I had clients that were heavily into short sales. They weren't that great at paying their CPA, but they had success in these transactions.

The term short sale just means that the offer to the lender is short of the amount due. In some states, the borrower may still be liable for the difference; however, many states have put in laws that relieve the borrower of any amounts due once the lender approves the short sale.

In my client's model, they would pay the current borrower and the lender an agreed-upon price to obtain the property. Other short sellers will pay the lender for the note and then do the foreclosure themselves to acquire the property. This latter variation keeps you from contacting the borrower, aside from the required filings and eventual auction. Since these notes are often more than five years old, there's a vast difference between what the investor is paying and the market value of the property.

CHAPTER 7

MANAGING REAL PROPERTY

Managing Yourself

I must say that I was not very good at seeing the signs that I needed to hire a property manager. My wife, Angela, was our property manager for the longest time. She would collect the rents, make the deposits, and fill out the leases. She—along with my executive assistant at the firm, who helped her— would handle the calls, show houses, and line up maintenance contractors.

We hummed along like that for a while. We had about thirty units and were looking at buying the infamous storage units. As stated before, I bought the first set without research and a clear understanding of what it takes to manage storage units. Then I bought the second set. I could feel the frustration building, with Angela trying to manage the phone and leasing. Between the two storage units, we had around 270 doors. (I can't remember the exact number.) With all that together, it was more than Angela wanted to deal with.

In hindsight, I should have hired a separate leasing agent for the storage units. All the processes and procedures were different. Angela was happy with the residential rental units. Managing them was fun for her. The storage units were a different beast.

One evening at home, I was relaxing on the couch watching TV and playing with the kids, when I heard my sweet wife curse the person on the other end of the phone and then throw the phone across the room. That is when I decided to hire a property manager.

I hope it doesn't come to that for you.

Managing property is not for the faint at heart. Most people who begin the real estate journey will opt to manage their rentals themselves. In truth, that is the best option, unless you have a full-time job that doesn't allow for the occasional variance from the nine-to-five workday. You learn a lot from managing property that you would never know by hiring someone else to do so.

If you make this decision, you must do your homework. You should know your state's property laws, the courts of eviction and small claims, the dates that trigger the eviction process, and who can appear before the court. Every state has its own variations of these laws, and it would serve you to learn them.

You might hire an attorney to walk through your first few evictions, noting the process and what they do and how they do it.

Go ahead and read the property code. It might not make sense while reading it, but when you are going through some dispute, you may begin to understand it a bit better.

When my daughter, Kate, took over as our property manager, she did all of this. She downloaded the property code that pertains to evictions, leases, and the like. She assembled them into a property management handbook that gave specific instructions on the process and what procedures would cover the property owner. We had a few conference calls with our attorney and his paralegal to ensure we were in compliance.

Remember, if you are treating this as a business, it helps to know the rules of the game.

When tenants get into the eviction process, they don't usually behave well. Sometimes they threaten lawsuits. It will happen. There may be a lawyer they know who is willing to write a letter to scare you into bending to their will. If you know the law and are familiar with the statutes, these letters will be little more than filler for the waste bin.

At twenty years old, Kate went to an eviction suite for some tenants who had stopped paying. They had brought a lawyer to argue for them. The justice of the peace wasn't impressed with the attorney's arguments, and since Kate had all her documents in place and followed the procedures outlined in the Texas property code, he ruled in our favor.

I guess they had the money to pay the attorney but didn't want to pay their rent? Whatever the case, being prepared and following the letter of the law can mean all the difference.

If you hire someone to manage your property, you won't get to know the process. And sometimes you have no choice. Managing your own property isn't necessary to build wealth with real estate, but it may be the only option for small upstarts.

There are some things you can do to make it easier to manage your property. Aside from doing your homework on the laws in your state, as mentioned, you may also want to apply the following tips outlined in this chapter.

Find and use property management software. There are many places to look for these, and they run the gambit on pricing and scalability. Find an affordable software that works for you and notifies you of things like sending out late notices, lease renewals, etc. Some software can even create your leases. All you need to do is input the tenant's name and contact information, rent and deposit amount, length of the lease, and it will do the rest. Some management applications also have a full general ledger accounting function. This is helpful if you know something about accounting, but most of the time, you should use the software in conjunction with another accounting software. I will talk more about using accounting software later.

Set up a separate bank account and credit cards for your rental activities. Later, we will talk about the possible legal entities you might consider for real estate investment. But for now, I assume that everything will be under your name. That is fine in the beginning. From the beginning, though, you should not mingle your rentals with your personal accounts. It is much easier to have these transactions separate from your groceries, gym membership, Amazon addictions, and the like when tax time comes around.

Keep an old-school spiral notebook planner/calendar. Sometimes the best tech is low tech. I keep both an electronic and paper calendar. The paper calendar helps me see the blocks of my schedule and remember appointments better. Some people color code and highlight and such; that isn't required, but it may be helpful to you. Rental properties are date-driven. Each month there are late notice dates, payment due dates (which should always be the first of the month), HVAC maintenance checks, filter checks, etc. Then annually, there are insurance renewals, real estate tax due dates, and tax return due dates—not to mention all the property showings and contractor meetings. This calendar/planner will help you map out your week.

Have a different cell phone number for the rentals. It isn't very expensive anymore to have a separate cell phone for your rentals. Some people prefer landlines, but it is best to have a cell phone for emergencies and showings. Later, when you hire a property manager, you can give them the phone instead of getting a new phone number for yourself.

Set a schedule for answering calls. For storage units, people will call pretty much 24/7. It is less that way for single-family rentals, but they will still call after hours expecting someone to answer. It is amazing to me that apartment complexes have posted hours that the manager will be available, and people stick to that. But for the landlord who manages their own properties, people don't respect the business hours as much. You will have to set a schedule of when you will answer calls and when you won't. My daughter's phone reminds her to turn the properties' phone off every day at 6:00 p.m. That is the schedule she decided on. You can choose whatever schedule works for you, but you should stick to it. What about emergencies and maintenance calls? I'm glad you asked...

Have a separate cell phone for emergencies. This is optional, of course. The cost of an additional cellphone may prohibit this practice. You might not answer it directly. Instead, listen to the messages immediately, and call back when appropriate. A clogged toilet may not be an emergency. Water flowing into the hall is. Screening the voicemails will help you decide. You will want to give your tenants a list of what qualifies as an emergency—which may include a list of examples. You should keep the ringer on to know when something is happening, and then listen to the voicemail. Another option may be an after-hours answering service that only calls you when something on the list of emergencies happens.

Automate the payment process. The world is different now than when we started. When I had to relocate to Irving, Texas, and had tenants in West Texas, I had to innovate a way to receive payments. Most tenants didn't want to send checks through the mail, so I gave them deposit slips for a checking account at a bank in both locations. They made the deposit by cash, money order, or checks. Today, you can set up a PayPal account, use ACH transactions, and even accept credit/debit cards. Note, however, that credit card companies have rules against using them for certain payments. Be sure not to break those rules when taking credit cards. If the automation doesn't work for you, I recommend a P.O. box or a box at a mail service center. I also would recommend that you don't have them drop payments off at your house, even if you have a dropbox-type mailbox.

These helpful hints are not mandatory, and depending on where you live, they may not be necessary.

Policies and Procedures

We have touched on having policies and procedures in place for managing properties. In the previous section, I laid out a few guidelines and practices that will help you get started. Here, I will share more about the importance of setting policies and procedures, and I will outline a few that you should follow. Note that I don't want to get into the weeds on specific policies and procedures, because your approach might be different from mine—along with the laws regarding the property codes and how landlords are supposed to behave.

You should have a policy manual. I'm surprised at how long I went without one. My real estate company was begun as a side business and didn't always get my full attention. However, when I hired my daughter as my property manager, that was the first thing she did. Until then, all that the manager did—and when he did it—was in his head. Also, he was very inconsistent with his execution of those policies. Subsequently, when Kate took over, she was surprised when all these deals were made with tenants as to when they paid and when they were considered late.

It was a mess to clean up, but she did it well. As I said before, we first figured out the legal rules and regulations from our conference call with the attorney and his paralegal. Then we received more information from the justices of the peace in our precincts about how they like things done (which unfortunately was not the same for each). Then we made some decisions about how we would proceed.

It is imperative that you apply the policies equally among all tenants. Once you set a policy in place, it shouldn't change unless it was grossly in error. If it needs to change, you should send a letter to all tenants notifying them of the change.

These policy changes cannot conflict with the lease agreements as written. So if the lease agreement needs to be amended or re-written, you will have to wait until the next renewal date or ask the tenant to sign an amendment to the lease. They do not have to sign any modification, especially if it is more stringent than the original lease.

If the laws change that affects the tenant, it is good to send out a notice of the change with a copy of the property code section. That isn't required, but it's still a good idea.

When policies are established, stay consistent. This trains your tenants to behave the way you want them to.

My father-in-law, Larry, was not the best property manager. He would listen to every sad story from the tenants. He would let tenants pay late, waive the late fee, and even allowed them to pay less than the agreed upon price. I don't remember how it was decided or who made the decision, but it was determined that Larry wouldn't talk to tenants any longer. My mother-in-law, Beth, would handle that from then on. She could be empathetic yet stick to the terms of the lease and the policies about when payments were late, reinforcing the late fee. She was compassionate yet firm. It was a better arrangement.

If you have the tendencies that Larry displayed, you probably should give up the title of property manager to another member of your household. Or you could hire one.

When to Hire a Property Manager

When Angela threw the phone across the room, I was awakened that it was time to hire a property manager. For our family, for her sanity, and for my peace, it had to be done.

First, we hired a real estate agent to be our property manager. As I shared, he was employed for both the residential rental and the storage units.

Unfortunately, the broker I hired later hired someone to handle my properties. And that guy had no experience with managing property.

I should have walked away at that point. But I didn't. Several problems came up after he took over.

First, as I've shared earlier in this book, the storage units need to be managed differently. There is no difference in the tenant's mind between my box and my competitor's box. The storage unit rental industry is a competitive landscape in some cities. The prices are set by the market, so everyone must run their operations very similarly in that respect. As stated earlier, when a potential tenant calls about your units, they are usually parked in front and just want you to come open one up for them. Or they load up and drive to the first open box. If you don't answer the phone, they will go to the next storage units on the list they pulled up from Google.

Our new property manager was managing our storage units like residential rental units. He would let all calls go to voicemail and then check the messages. By the time he called them back, they'd already signed with someone else.

I kept telling him he had to answer the phone. We even got a separate number for storage units, in order to know which one must be answered. He just wouldn't answer them. I figure he cost us about $12,000 in lost rents in the six months he managed the units.

Another problem is that he didn't screen tenants like Angela had done for the residential rental houses. During his six months, we had more late payments, partial payments, and no payments than we'd ever had.

Eventually, I had to release him and figure out something else. In Texas, you must be a licensed real estate agent to manage property for someone for whom you are not an owner, an attorney, related by family, or an employee. So, we opted to hire someone in-house who I could directly manage. This worked out much better, and we continued to grow and add more houses to our portfolio.

Hopefully, this book helps you learn from my mistakes. One of the mistakes that I made at this point is that the property manager was also our maintenance manager. Up until around the sixty-five-unit mark, it worked well. But when I bought thirty-seven units at one time, and suddenly I was over one hundred units, it was clear that the property manager/ maintenance manager model wasn't working. Neither job was getting done with excellence.

It wasn't the property manager's fault; it was his boss's fault for not recognizing that it was too much to ask. Because the growth happened rapidly, we hadn't taken the time to discuss the responsibilities of the positions and how to manage them. In hindsight (again), I would have hired a separate mainte- nance manager at around the sixty-unit mark. Then when we acquired the big package, all responsibilities would have been spread out, and we could have better managed the growth.

So how does that story help you? You just learned what *not* to do.

In business and other endeavors, I learned the principle of *scalability*. I'm not sure if this is written anywhere else, but I realized that no matter what we're doing—managing property or managing a CPA firm—we need to set up our processes and procedures, systems, and people to handle a 50 to 100 percent increase in overall operations.

What do I mean? When we managed thirty units, we need- ed to have our processes, procedures, people, and systems ready to handle sixty units. If you do this evaluation regularly, you'll never be at maximum capacity.

Again, the focus is on the *policies, procedures,* and *systems.* The *people* component might be limited by your revenues or availability. Professional property managers, for example, usually charge around 10 percent of the gross rents, plus other reletting fees. Your people question in relation to a property manager can be answered by the cost of hiring someone, full or part-time, in proportion to 10 percent of your gross rents. For maintenance personnel, it should be considered in proportion with the percentage of gross rents and the frequency of the demand. That percentage may be different based on the type of property you maintain. The number of units you have also plays a role. The more doors, the more potential issues, the greater the regularity of the work. Whatever you do, count the costs and be sure you can afford to hire before you hire.

Accounting and Reporting

As an accountant, I'd say that I'm an expert on this subject. Especially for real estate, you need an expert to help you account for these transactions.

Tools can also help. As I mentioned, there are many rental real estate software packages that you can buy to help you manage rentals as well as report the income and expenses for your CPA at the end of the year. We recommend using a cloud-based accounting software, if you haven't bought software with management and accounting capabilities already.

With QuickBooks, we recommend listing the property (not the individual) as the customer. This way, income and expenses can be allocated to the property. Reports then can be generated that will show how much each property is earning and costing you.

You can also use a *class* tracking function, if available, to show the income and expense per property where the property is a class. We use the class to differentiate between our commercial and residential rental properties.

I can't teach you all you need to know about accounting in this chapter. There are classes you can take for basic accounting skills. If you have more than twenty properties, you're probably better off hiring a professional. Since most of my clients who have multiple rental properties are cost sensitive, I understand if you feel like you need to do this yourself. Well, at least I think I understand.

During the year, you should give your accountant access to your cloud-based accounting system to monitor transactions and make sure they are appropriately categorized. This function will help you predict your taxes and cash flow along the way, instead of at the beginning of the next year when it is too late to do anything about it.

Accounting for real estate has several purposes. One is to forecast cash-flow. The second is to predict tax liabilities. Also, it allows you to manage certain expenses per property.

Cash flow, as we've discussed several times in this book, is the net cash after cash expenses, property improvements, and debt service. If you're looking at the income statement produced by your accountant, it will not display your cash flow. You must add back any depreciation taken, then subtract out your debt principal payments. Also, if you made any improvements, you would have to subtract those costs as well. Most accounting systems have a "statement of cash flows" in their report templates. It can be helpful, but sometimes it can be confusing to the untrained eye.

Many reports can be generated to give you valuable, meaningful information about your real estate investments. The important thing to remember is to have something that you can use for management, your accountant, and your lenders.

Since most deals happen quickly, waiting until the lender/underwriter asks you to provide an income statement is not the time to begin. The cost of losing a deal most often outweighs the cost of paying your accountant to keep your books up to date. From a management perspective, you should review at least monthly statements less than ten days out from the end of the month. That's not a must-have, but it is definitely a "should do."

Key Performance Indicators

Set up your accounting information to track and measure your portfolio's performance. *Key performance indicators* (KPIs) are measurements chosen that indicate if a business, business department, or property is performing as expected, better than expected, or worse than expected. They can be selected for the entire operation or a part of the operation.

For example, you might track the number of late payments per month. This would indicate the quality of tenants and your screening or collection process in general.

You may choose from an infinite number of KPIs. Whatever you decide to track should be meaningful to you and help determine if you are moving towards your goals. You might track items of income and expenses as a percentage of gross rents.

Some KPIs might be a combination of financial and non-financial data—like *net income per unit* (net income divided by the number of rental units).

The following table provides a list of possible KPIs specific to real estate. Your accountant may have standard financial ratios covered with their monthly reporting. Don't stop there.

KPI	Description	How It's Useful
Gross margin	Debt service/ gross rents	Cash flow margin before expenses
Debt service coverage ratio (DSCR)	Gross rents/ debt service	Number of times gross rents cover debt payments
Net income per unit or Gross rents per unit	Net income/ number of units or Gross rents/ number of units	Net income per unit or Gross income per unit
Loan to value	Total debt/fair market value of property	Percentage of borrowing available or net worth per property
Vacancy percentage	Number of vacancies/total number of units	Lost revenue, capacity
Days on market	Number of days available for rent	Lease advertised may be too high, property needs attention
Rent per square foot	Amount of rent/ square feet of property	Comparing properties in various markets

Payback period	Initial capital/ annual earnings from property	How long it should take to make back in earnings what you invested to purchase the property
Average mortgage rate	Sum of mortgage rates/number of mortgages	Average mortgage rate across all of your properties, assess refinancing or new purchases
Tenant turnover	Number of tenants moved out/total number of tenants	Rate at which your tenants are leaving
Capitalization Rate	Gross annual rent/total cost of property	Return on investment

These, again, are just a few of the KPIs that might be helpful to you as a real estate investor. These should only be used after you have decided on your specific goals for investing in real estate. You may create new KPIs that are directly related to those goals. After using one KPI to track a goal, you may find that a different KPI is a better indicator of your progress.

KPIs are like the box scores in baseball. Certain statistics are useful to assess individuals or how you did each inning. However, the statistic that matters most after the game is the score. It shows you if you won or lost the game. The other stats show you *how* you won or lost the game.

I would recommend finding one main KPI that says, "We are winning!" Then use the other KPIs to help determine where you need to focus your attention. To use the baseball analogy again, what is the team's on-base percentage? How many players are left on base at the end of each inning? Where are the weaknesses in the lineup? These all show *how* you are winning or losing but not *whether* you are winning or losing.

The good thing for you is that real estate investing doesn't last just nine innings. You never get to a point where you simply have won or lost. Some people say that they have lost in real estate, but in truth, they probably just forfeited the game. They may have given up after a few tries or, like some financial gurus who have become famous, lost big because of mistakes and/or hubris, then never got back in the game.

Many of my martial arts instructors have said this about losing: "There are not winners and losers here at the tournament; there are only winners and learners." Every day managing real estate or any business, you learn.

CHAPTER 8

NAVIGATING OPPORTUNITY INDIGESTION

Opportunities Will Come

When I was going into the sixth grade, I signed up for band. Not because I wanted to be in band, but instead to get out of the piano lessons I'd been forced into since the third grade.

Before school started, I walked into the band hall with my dad to pick an instrument. There were so many to choose from: clarinets, trumpets, French horns, oboes, percussion, snare drums, tubas, and an assortment of stringed instruments.

For an eleven-year-old, it was opportunity overload. In my mind, whatever decision I made, that was it. If I chose oboe, then I was stuck with it. I now play several different instruments, including the piano (which is my favorite now). But then, it seemed so final.

I was leaning towards the drums, but my dad (who didn't want to hear me beating on the drums all day) steered me away. Instead, I landed on the trombone. I think my dad was equally dismayed at this choice. Even now, I regret not following my heart on that occasion.

There is no such thing as a once-in-a-lifetime opportunity. If you are looking for them, they come around all the time. Some are better than others. It is up to you to determine which ones are worth investing in. Someone once said that you are more likely to die of *indigestion of opportunities* rather than from *starvation.*

What is an opportunity? In real estate, opportunities come from market swings, changes in buyer behavior, local industry booms, etc. But how do you recognize them? What do they look like? Each person has a different perspective when looking at properties. They look with the eyes of their experience and talents. An opportunity for one might be a money pit for someone else.

When looking at various opportunities, don't compare yourself to others. You must see the reality of your capital, capacity, strengths, and timing. I've passed on many properties because I know my limitations and talents. I know what I can manage and what I can't.

If there's an opportunity in a new real estate type, you might start small and see if you can develop the skills necessary to go bigger later. I define an opportunity by the four areas mentioned above; capital, capacity, strengths, and timing. Here are the four questions you should ask yourself before you take on a real estate investment:

First, ask yourself, *do I have the capital necessary to acquire and maintain this property?* The "capital necessary" includes the down payment, monthly mortgage payment, and money for possible repairs and improvements. You should be able to handle each new property from your current assets and cash flow as if the new property would not bring in any additional income. Also, the new property or properties shouldn't be a significant portion of your current net capital. If you have $1 million in net capital, anything that will require more than 30 percent of that capital is not an opportunity. It is a gamble. I am not saying I haven't made that gamble before. But it was a significant risk to my business and our personal assets. It can work out, but don't call that an opportunity. You might as well go to Vegas.

Second, ask, *do I have the capacity needed to manage the property?* If the capital requirement is less than 30 percent of your net capital, great. Now, who will manage it? If you have hired an in-house property manager and have a repair and maintenance crew, do they have the capacity to add additional units to their jobs? *Your* time is also limited. Consider what the new investment will take of your time. From the initial purchase to assignments of your management team, a new property will consume more time. Even though someone once told you, "You make time for your priorities," you cannot make more time. Land and time are resources we cannot manufacture.

Third, ask, *does this opportunity exploit my strengths and avoid my weaknesses in real estate?* This is an alignment issue. The property should be in direct complement to your strengths. I will say more about this in the section regarding staying within your model. When you determine whether perceived opportunities are actual opportunities for you, list your strengths in property management, property types, systems, and processes. Then see if those strengths are magnified with the acquisition of this property.

Fourth, ask, *is this the right time for this opportunity?* This is a hard one. It is both wise and gut-wrenching to pass on a property because it is not the right time. I used to tell my wife that I would never tell her no if she wanted something. I would merely say, "Not right now." That worked for a little while. The only way it really works is if you understand why *now* is not the right time. It could be because the market is too volatile. It could be that you have several other properties or projects to which you have committed. Whatever the reason, you must map out some questions or criteria that determine what makes it the right time.

My acquaintances in real estate used to say, "You don't steal in slow motion!" This means that if something is a steal—a bargain opportunity—you must move fast, or it won't be a steal much longer. So, once you have decided that something is, in fact, an opportunity, it's time to move on it! Don't hesitate. You have carefully evaluated the property; you've asked these four questions. It's time to pull the trigger—or walk away!

Discipline: The Bridge Between Desire and Delight

Crap! Someone said the D-word! It isn't a four-letter word, but it sometimes has the same shocking response: *discipline*. What is discipline, and how is it applied to real estate investing? The question seems straightforward, but it undoubtedly isn't.

Many years ago, I heard a pastor preach a sermon on discipline. He said, "First comes desire, then discipline is applied, and finally therein is delight." Aside from the crafty alliteration, there was a tremendous amount of truth laid out in that sermon. Everyone starts out wanting to do something. We see this very clearly in children. Then, we see its downfall in a lack of follow-through.

Parents will say to a friend who has become proficient in playing the guitar, "I wish my parents would have made me play an instrument." Then later, sometimes in the same conversation, they will say, "I tried to get Johnny to play piano, but he just didn't like practicing, so we quit." Oh, the irony!

Discipline is the activity, exercise, or regimen that develops or improves a skill. When used as a verb, according to Dictionary.com, it is defined as: *the act of training by instruction and exercise; to bring to a state of order and obedience by training and control.* No wonder no one really likes the word! It just feels oppressive when you say it.

The truth is more encouraging than the dictionary leads you to believe. First, there is no such thing as discipline if there is no *vision*. Desire comes first. The child, parent, or student first must *want* to learn. If a child doesn't want to read, there are ways to show them the benefits of reading and then help produce that desire.

With music training, the first discussion you have with a kid interested in playing an instrument or learning vocal training is digging deep into the *why*. We talked about this in chapter four. One day, I talked to my son about why he wanted to play the piano on the way to his music lesson. At first, he only could communicate his love for music. We started there.

"It is great that you love music, but how does that make you want to learn to play the piano?"

As I kept probing, I got to his vision statement: "I want to learn to create music and share it with others, so they can be happy like I am when I listen to music."

Remember, he was ten when this conversation went down. Pretty deep for a ten-year-old. He still complains when we want him to practice, or when it is time to go to a lesson. However, now I just remind him of what he said. I'm not demanding him to do something I want him to do. Instead, I'm reminding him why he really wants to do this. And it helps him—although sometimes with pouting—to push through and do it.

When I began to learn guitar, it was just the same. I had a vision, and that kept me practicing.

You see the same thing in skate parks—kids working hours tirelessly on tricks. They have a vision, and it produces discipline.

So how does this concept apply to investing in real estate? Your vision will guide you in making decisions. When you map out what is important to you and the model you have chosen, the choices become easier when opportunities come. You have a standard on which to gauge all opportunities. You aren't merely being held accountable by your CPA, although they can help if you express your vision and have regular conversations.

The business coaching we offer to entrepreneurs does this. We don't set the direction and vision of your company for you; you do it, with our guidance. We act as an accountability partner to help in your decision-making process. Sometimes we might use tools to help get you there. But all the criteria and standards come from you, our client.

The worst thing we can do is answer the question, "What would you do in our situation?" I know clients sometimes want me to decide for them, but my answer won't be the same as your answer. Why? My vision isn't the same as your vision. Even if our goals are the same, my values, strengths and weaknesses, mission, resources, and experience are different from yours.

Discipline is the bridge that brings you from that vision, *desire*, or mission, to true fulfillment or *delight*.

As I mentioned before, discipline works best with an accountability partner. If you have decided you will do something or pursue a strategy, tell your team and those to whom you report. Ask them to hold you accountable to that strategy or goal.

Accountability only works when someone holds you to what *you* have set as a goal. You can't hold someone responsible for your goals or strategies and expect enthusiasm or follow-through. That is the old command-and-control type of leadership. That method of leadership won't get you or your team to its full potential. What it will do is breed resentment and burnout.

Whether you or your team needs more discipline, remember it is just the bridge to something greater. Start with the vision, and then see how everything changes.

Growth Budget

Growth doesn't usually happen by accident.

We grow up with some expectations of growth. When we are kids, growth happens without putting in any effort. It is expected, and it can be very disappointing when it doesn't happen—especially if you hope to play basketball or football in college.

Unfortunately, after your natural growth has ended, the natural state of things is to move towards decline. That is true in business as well. The business growth curve moves from start-up to growth to plateau and eventually decline.

If you want to grow in your real estate investing, it should be planned and budgeted. Starting out, you may not have any growth goals in mind. Just cash flow. Or maybe just increasing your net worth. We talked some about this in the entrepreneurial mindset chapter.

In this chapter, my purpose is to warn you about growing too fast. It isn't easy to grow, but when you feel momentum start moving and driving you, it takes a lot of effort and discipline to stay within your growth budget.

Your *growth budget* is the amount of growth that you can effectively handle, increasing your cash flow. What may surprise many is that growth can actually reduce cash flow. In business and economics, we call this *economies of scale*. It is where one additional unit produced begins to decrease cash flow.

How is that possible? With real estate, it happens when you need to hire another person to manage or maintain property. Or when additional units require a change in the process, increasing your costs.

For example, you have been managing property with Excel spreadsheets. That is fine for now, but how would your process need to change if you were to buy five more properties? What is the cost of the software necessary to manage your property? Would you also need to hire someone to enter data or hire your CPA firm to help you in accounting? In these cases, the increase in units has decreased your overall percentage of cash flow per unit. As you continue to grow, your average cash flow per unit increases, as those costs are now spread over the additional units.

Growth must also be budgeted to keep your cash flow positive and within your budget targets. At the beginning of the year or sometime during the year, decide how many additional properties you can add without adding staff or changing your process. Depending on your business model, that may be in terms of additional properties, storage unit buildings, or apartment complexes. Then, like a baseball player, look for your pitch. Don't swing at junk. Don't go after properties that are outside of the budget. Take swings at good properties; even if you don't end up closing on them, you will feel better about the process when you know you were in the strike zone.

Too many baseball analogies? I didn't think so either. The point is, you don't have to swing at every pitch. There will be decent properties that you will have to pass on.

I watched the College World Series recently, and the pitchers for Mississippi State were striking out most of the University of Texas hitters throughout the game. The starter and closer for MSU had twenty-one strikeouts between them when it ended. There are only twenty-seven outs in a nine-inning game. It was a new College World Series record.

In the third or fourth inning, one of the announcers said that the starting pitcher for MSU used a combination of low and away sliders and high fastballs to close most of the strikeouts. The UT hitters couldn't lay off of them, and they couldn't hit them either.

You will lose the game if you don't pass on these out-of-budget opportunities. You could get over-leveraged, not understand the increase in costs with the additional units, and lose money. This may not bankrupt you, but it will put a lot of pressure on your margins. Unfortunately, from experience, when this happens, you just have to live with it until you can sell off some units or your processes get normalized, and you have economies of scale again.

Baseball explains most areas of life and business. I may use another baseball analogy again. You have been warned.

Stay Within the Model

If you set your budget and know what you can add each year without rocking the boat and eating up additional cash flow, the last area in which to remain disciplined is staying within your model.

To refresh your memory, as we discussed in the chapter about an entrepreneurial mindset, when determining your model, you should ask the following five questions:

1. *What type of investment property works best for us?*
2. *What price range makes sense for us and is within our budget?*
3. *What areas are we most familiar with, and how can we leverage that knowledge?*
4. *How will we evaluate properties in the future?*
5. *What type of property will we say no to?*

These five questions help to define your business model in real estate investing. You could probably ask some more questions that would drill down even further.

I was coaching a business owner, Kathy, about her storage unit business, and she'd asked the question: "Should I sell or continue to own and build more units on this site?" It is a question that everyone in business asks themselves at one point or the other. She had gotten several offers per year, after building several buildings, and had plans to add two more.

I asked her, "Why do they want to buy your units?"

The answer was shocking, "Because essentially, they want to be *you*, Kathy." I explained that they wanted a good, cash flowing, easy to operate, high net worth business to invest in—as she'd become known for.

She'd found her model. The next question is whether she could recreate the same thing at another location, or even in another state.

The answer is *yes*. Because she'd done it once, I thought she could do the same thing several times.

The first inclination was to *go big*. Recreate what she had. But after some careful thought about how she'd managed to build her current investment, we determined that starting small, as she'd done before, was the best move. Her model was *slow and steady growth in building storage units, leasing, and managing the business.* She was good at it and had learned the industry very well.

Staying within your model is the best way to grow in a steady, disciplined manner. As I've said, our niche is residential real estate. Someday I might get into multi-family properties. Before I do, I would need to research and prepare—also starting small to see if we can do it and do it well.

There is no wisdom in going out and buying a two-hundred-unit apartment complex if you have not managed a twenty-four-unit complex first. There are always properties available that allow you to scale up to your goals. Gateway properties allow you to learn the process before launching into the deep.

Let's explore each of the five questions to gain an understanding of your model.

Property Type

What type of property works best for us? Most individual investors begin with single-family residential rentals. Some like investing in raw land, holding for a while, then selling for gain. What works best for you has a lot to do with the market around you, your need for cash flow, and financing.

If you don't have good credit, buying land or tax foreclosures might be a good alternative. You must pay cash, but it is at such a significant discount you can pull it off without borrowing.

Answering this question also has to do with risk. How much risk are you willing to endure? It may be that mobile homes or lot rentals appeal to you because the cash upfront is so low.

The more cash in the game means less risk of future earnings being used to pay a mortgage. I know a couple that only pays cash for middle to upper-middle-class single-family homes. They don't own many properties, but their net worth and cash flow are high because they have no debt. This takes some serious saving on the front end but has excellent results on the back end. For them, debt is a risk they don't want.

Price Range

What price range makes sense for us and is in our budget? Choosing a price range arbitrarily can slow your growth in real estate investing. Knowing beforehand your sweet spot in investing helps you move quickly on properties. Again, you don't steal in slow motion.

It is best to have all the criteria for property worked out before you shop. It is like going to the grocery store without a list; you spend too much and get home with crap you can't use. What makes sense for you isn't the same as what makes sense for others. I know I could buy land and re-plat it for small ranchettes, but should I? No, I don't have the time needed to go into that kind of investing. Yet this model is very profitable for a client of mine. He's a helicopter pilot, which makes viewing potential properties a bit easier and more fun.

Familiar Areas

What areas are we most familiar with, and how can we leverage that knowledge? I like investing in small, rural-based communities close to more industrial areas. I find the tenants and properties suit me well. You might be more familiar with condos in urban areas. Or beachfront property in Florida. That is where you start.

After you get a nice portfolio of properties built up, it wouldn't hurt to try some other markets. But start small. Betting big doesn't always work in Vegas either. When you get familiar with a local market, you begin to understand what works and what doesn't in that market. Taking what you know about that market and looking for similar markets in other cities and states may be a good way to leverage what you have learned. No two markets are the same, but they may have similarities that can be exploited to your advantage.

We invest in a college town with an Air Force base, for a number of reasons. First, the number of eighteen-to-twenty-five-year-olds needing housing is pretty high, and the population is fluid. We also found out that if you rent to an airman, any issues you have with that tenant can be resolved quickly by visiting with his commanding officer (CO). An airman and their family will always leave their unit in better shape than they found it, which is probably the same for the other branches. Not to mention that the standards of cleanliness and order while living in our units are high for active military. We love our veterans and those serving; active military are some of the best tenants to have.

Looking Forward

How will we evaluate properties in the future? You set the criteria before starting this real estate investing game. Now, what have you learned? Before, you were just beginning this life of the real estate entrepreneur. Now, you have some purchases under your belt. What can you do better next time? A continuous improvement mindset answers these questions.

A mistake some investors make is writing off a type of property because of a bad experience, like me and storage units. I can't say that I'll never invest in storage units again, but now I know more of what it takes and how to manage them. I'd first have to convince my wife that it was a good idea. But whether you have my kind of experience or not, you should be cataloging your experience and discussing these four helpful questions with your partners, spouse, or yourself:

1. *What went right?*
2. *What went wrong?*
3. *What was missing?*
4. *What was confused?*

These questions help you evaluate your experience, turn that experience into knowledge, and wisely apply that knowledge for future purchases.

One other thing I learned was that I needed to manage my expectations with lenders. Lenders want to help. Your mortgage broker wants the loan to happen, but must answer to underwriters. I am a type A person who is generally impatient. All of my issues here have to do with expectations. My life and relationships are better when I set more realistic and accurate expectations on myself, the lenders, buyers, and sellers.

How will you evaluate properties in the future, now that you have begun the investing process?

Saying No!

What type of property will we say no to? Do you have a *stop doing* list? You should.

One of my stop-doing items is "stop buying dog properties just because you can." Even if the property meets all the criteria you set, some properties are just on the "don't buy" list. The properties you say no to will help you improve your inventory.

Sometimes the house you should have said no to is already in your inventory. We had several homes in a housing development twenty minutes outside of town. All other criteria were met. We didn't realize that a property so far outside of town without any supplies stores nearby made it very difficult to maintain. To prune our inventory, I offered those properties to another buyer at my cost just to lighten our load and help our maintenance crew focus on properties within our service area. The other investor already had a crew that lived out there, and it worked really well for him. The decision to cull our list wasn't easy, but it had to be done for our growth. Now, the out-of-town properties are on the don't buy list. At least for that city.

When you invest in other cities, it's good to consider proximity to supplies and vendors who will help you maintain them.

We have discussed at length now what it means to stay in your model and live without opportunity indigestion. The next chapter will discuss the best ways to own real estate.

CHAPTER 9

EXPLORING FORMS OF OWNERSHIP

Types of Entities

As a staff accountant in a small firm in San Angelo, Texas, I have met some interesting characters. One of the strangest meetings I attended with my former boss was with a real estate investor looking for a CPA.

Over lunch at a favorite Mexican food place, he began to spell out his real estate investing strategy and structure. Now, I had only just started my real estate empire, so I was very interested in how others were making their way to real estate wealth. This guy was a retired professional who had begun investing twenty years prior.

To my surprise, he spun before us a tangled web of trusts and LLCs used to conceal his income from the IRS and shelter himself from **all** potential liability created from owning property. While he spoke, I remembered the "dirty dozen" list the IRS posts on their website each year. It's a list of the twelve most egregious tax scams discovered during audits the prior year. I think he may have been employing more than one on the list in his enterprise. By the end of the lunch, I knew that I didn't want anything to do with that client. That "creative investor" was engaging in tax evasion, which is illegal.

Owning real estate in trusts and LLCs for liability protection is a familiar and sound business practice. We will discuss the right way to own real estate to maximize your tax benefits and help protect your personal assets from liability.

As you build your real estate empire, you might consider changing how you own that real estate. Before, I have mentioned using a limited partnership to create a syndicate of investors to finance—in part or in full—the purchase of a package of properties or an apartment complex. This chapter will discuss the types of entities available, what works best for real estate, how to use multiple entities together, and some passive versus active types of income generated by real estate.

Choosing the right entity can protect your assets from creditors and taxes. This is where you need to rely on your team to help you navigate these various types of entities.

Individually Owned

Generally, most people get started buying real estate individually. If you only have a few small properties, this type of ownership is perfectly acceptable. All of your income in expenses from the rental of those properties will be reported on Schedule E of your Form 1040, US Individual Income Tax Return. Schedule E gives insight into what types of expenses you need to track, and your tax advisor will help you with any expenses not included on the form.

This ownership type is simple and doesn't require you to file anything with the state, county, or Internal Revenue Service (IRS), aside from Schedule E. You don't have to create a separate bank account, although I highly recommend that you do.

The downside is that you are personally responsible for any liability that might arise from owning that property. Asset protection includes the use of insurance, but it also includes using limited liability entities like LLCs, corporations, limited partnerships, and trusts. We will discuss these options next.

Partnerships

Partnerships are a form of ownership with two or more owners. They can be general partnerships, limited liability partnerships, or limited partnerships—each with its own positive and negative liability shield and tax treatment.

General Partnerships

General partnerships are entities with two or more partners who share the partnership's liability. They can be created by filing an assumed name certificate with the county clerk in the county you intend on doing business. No state filings are required, since it has no liability shield. I do not recommend using this type of partnership. Real estate is just about the only type of business that might use a general partnership, unless the partners are all limited liability entities themselves.

Limited Liability Partnerships (LLPs)

Limited liability partnerships (LLPs) are similar to general partnerships except that the partners are only liable for their own actions. Generally, this arrangement is used by a group of professionals, like attorneys and accountants. Two limited liability entities can use it to form a joint venture for a short time. LLPs are created by filing a registration statement with the secretary of state of your state. In Texas, they must be renewed on a recurring basis. Other limited liability entities are perpetual and not required to renew their registration.

Limited Partnerships (LPs)

Limited partnerships (LPs) have at least one general partner and at least one limited partner. The general partner is liable for all the partnership debts, whereas the limited partners are not. Also, the general partner controls the decisions and management of the partnership. Limited partners cannot demand a distribution, but their ownership interest has some protection against creditors. Usually, the general partner is a limited liability entity, like an LLC or a corporation. These are often used for estate planning purposes, since the limited partnership interest will receive a value discount in the estate. Talk to your estate planning attorney about how to use these partnerships.

Limited Liability Company (LLC)

The most popular form of ownership right now is the *limited liability company* (LLC). The LLC provides the owners with a liability shield on the owner's personal assets, much like a corporation. It is simple to create and manage. The owners of an LLC are called "members," and the default taxation by the IRS, if there are multiple members, is as a partnership. A single-member LLC is called a "disregarded entity." Don't you wish that were true? Disregarded in this sense means that the entity and the individual are the same for tax reporting purposes. The single-member LLC income and expenses are reported on Schedule E if the entity has passive rental income. Suppose the single-member LLC is an active trade or business. In that case, its income and expenses are reported on Schedule C. If that trade or business is a farming activity, that belongs on Schedule F. I don't want to spend any time on these other schedules except to say that you could possibly have the same SMLLC on multiple schedules, if the activities inside the entity were active, passive, or farming activity. For the love of God and all that is holy, don't do that. Separate your activities by entity or individual. Was that a strong enough recommendation? All the CPAs of the country can send their thank you notes to my email address referenced in the last chapter of this book.

Active Trade or Business Versus Passive Activity

What do I mean by *passive versus active trade or business*? This classification of income determines how the income is treated for tax purposes. An active trade or business, like plumbing or insurance, creates ordinary income. This is where it gets tricky. Sometimes that ordinary income also has self-employment tax rates applied to it. When the owner of the LLC interest has active participation, the income is subject to both federal income tax and self-employment taxes. If the LLC member is a "passive" member, then the ordinary income of the LLC is not subject to self-employment taxes. It is confusing, because the code uses similar words to describe passive versus active trade or business income and passive versus active participation of the LLC member or partner. One set of rules applies to the type of income, and another set of rules applies to the role of the LLC member or partner. I know this can be muddling to wade through, but don't worry. Instead, trust me when I say that you need a competent, enlightened CPA to handle the distinctions.

The IRS tax code generally considers LLC members and limited partners passive, but this doesn't make the income passive. Why is that important? You didn't ask because you have an awesome CPA who knows this crap, but I'll tell you anyway, in case you are still tracking with me. Passive losses cannot be used to offset ordinary income if your adjusted gross income is over a certain threshold. If the losses are not allowed, you have passive loss carryovers.

There are a few exceptions to the passive loss rules. They depend on the number of active participation hours and whether or not you are a real estate professional. Again, I hate getting into the weeds on the technical part of real estate taxation for this book.

Also, an LLC may be subject to state income taxes. In the great state of Texas, and a few other states, we do not have a state individual income tax. Our property taxes are crazy high, but we have no state income tax. The LLC *is* subject to state franchise "margin tax," which technically isn't income tax.

Partnership or Corporate Taxation

When you have multiple members of an LLC, you are required to file a partnership return. You can make an election to be taxed as a corporation or an S-corporation, but we will talk about that later. Let's assume that you were smart, and for your real estate entity, you chose *not* to make that election. Each member of the LLC can be actively or passively involved with the LLC. This matters for making an election to be treated as a real estate professional. Rental real estate is a passive activity, so it's not subject to self-employment tax. Otherwise, passive losses may be limited based on your adjusted gross income. Ask your tax advisor what that is and how you can avoid passive losses being suspended.

Real Estate Professional

Without getting too technical, any losses incurred as a real estate professional can be used to offset ordinary income on your tax return, not subject to limitation. To be classified as a real estate professional, you don't need to have a license; you just must accrue a certain number of hours of active management. There is also a level just below real estate professional called "active participation." It also has a number of hours threshold to get that preferential tax treatment.

What do you mean by "number of hours"? Is that per property, or all the properties aggregated? That is on a property-by-property basis.

What? That's stupid!

Yes, it is. You can make an election that will treat all of your rental real estate activities as one activity. This has pros and cons. Again, talk to your tax advisor. Real estate is one of the most complex areas of the tax code. You need an advisor. I mentioned that in the first chapter, and I'm saying it again in this chapter—multiple times—to be sure it's clear.

Corporations and S-Corporations

Corporations and *S-corporations* are another type of legal liability-shielding entity. They are more challenging to set up and have more rigid operational requirements.

Corporations are taxed at the corporate level, and if dividends are paid to the shareholders, they are taxed at the shareholder level as well. This is commonly known as double taxation. Earnings are taxed and then taxed again.

S-corporations, like partnerships, are "flow-through" entities. Earnings are not taxed at the corporate level, but as they flow through to their shareholders, they are taxed there.

I don't recommend owning real estate in corporations, S or otherwise. There are many limitations and tax issues with corporations that you won't have with the partnership rules. With S-corporations, the shareholder must be an employee of the company and take a "reasonable" salary. This means that you are turning passive income into ordinary income and creating payroll taxes for yourself. Not generally the wisest move.

There are some instances where owning real property in a corporation might have non-tax benefits, but you would need to get a complete understanding with your tax advisor to do so. Also, when you contribute real property to a partnership, let's say a husband-and-wife partnership, and then later take that real property out, there is no tax consequence. The transaction is recorded at historical cost, where the basis in the hands of the partners is the same as the basis in the hands of the partnership, as long as the ownership stays the same coming out as it went in.

On the other hand, with a corporation, you can contribute real property to the corporation without a tax consequence.

However, if you were to distribute that property to the same shareholders, you would need to record that as a dividend or sale at the property's fair market value.

There are some exceptions and other tax considerations here, so you need to consult with your tax advisor. Tax planning is beyond the scope of this book. What is important is that, generally, you should hold appreciating property, like real estate, in an LLC taxed as a partnership.

Multiple Entities

Real estate investors commonly use *multiple entities*. Many variations can be seen in the wild, but I will mention just a few. Since this book is geared toward the entrepreneur looking for additional passive income, I will focus on scenarios that would be most useful.

Limited Partnership (again)

We discussed the limited partnership. It is a partnership consisting of at least one general partner and at least one limited partner. The general partner is fully liable for partnership liabilities. In contrast, the limited partner's liabilities are limited to their investment in the partnership.

Often, the general partner is another limited liability entity. You can use an S-corporation, corporation, or another LLC for the general partner to assure that your personal assets are shielded from partnership debts.

How much of the limited partnership must a general partner own? That is a good question. The only limitation that Texas places on the general partner is that there be at least one. The ownership interest can be a fraction of a percentage. In practice, it is best for the general partner to have the smallest percentage of ownership; I often use 1 percent. In addition, the general partnership interest and limited partnership interest can be owned by the same person or entity.

I can feel minds being blown.

My wife and I can hold a 1 percent general partnership interest and 49.5 percent limited partnership interest each. We don't, but it is possible. I prefer the general partner to be an entity and the limited partners to be individuals, but that is just a preference.

Many estate planning attorneys use limited partnerships in various functions, and through inheritance and planning, heirs could end up with both types of ownership interest over time.

Series LLCs

Another use of multiple entities is *series LLCs*. Series LLCs are only allowed in a few states. Texas is one of those states, as are Illinois, Iowa, Nevada, Oklahoma, Tennessee, Utah, and the territory of Puerto Rico. You might be able to register in the other states to do business there with a series LLC, but that is beyond the scope of this book.

The benefit of the series LLC is that you only have to create your formation documents once. Then when you need another LLC in the series, you create one by amending the operating agreement to include the new series. Each LLC in the series is only liable for its own debts, and all are controlled by the master LLC.

The benefit for the real estate investor is that you can segregate properties in their own LLC without creating a new entity.

You must treat each LLC as a separate company, including income, expenses, operations, etc. You need an independent management company to keep things separate without opening separate bank accounts for each series. Since there are no organizational documents for each of the new LLCs, you can't open a bank account for them. Look to your real estate attorney to help sort out the best way to use these entities.

As mentioned, you may need to hire a property manager to manage the properties deeded to series LLCs. You can create a corporation, or an LLC taxed as a corporation, to be the manager; or you can hire an outside property manager.

If you are managing the property in-house, setting up a separate entity to do so might be the best method to handle the day-to-day operations of your real estate investments.

Land Trusts

Another way some real estate investors have used different entities is by creating a *land trust* with an LLC as the beneficiary. A trust is created when a grantor or settlor contributes property to a trustee to manage for the benefit of one or more beneficiaries. I won't go into the hows and whys to using a trust, but it is an option.

There are *revocable* and *irrevocable trusts*. Revocable trusts are considered grantor trusts, where the trust income is reported on the grantor's tax return. There are still creditor protections, but a tax return for the trust may not be filed.

The use of trusts can be a way to remain anonymous in your real estate investing. The trustee can be an individual or an entity. Nevada and Wyoming both allow members of an LLC to stay anonymous as well. Paired together, the land trust with a Wyoming LLC as trustee and as the beneficiary would shelter an individual's investments to prying eyes. I'm not recommending this level of paranoia, but it is available to those who fear lawsuits from unscrupulous attorneys. Again, please consult your invaluable attorney for guidance on this type of asset protection. This chapter has been so hard to write. Sometimes the most important parts of owning real estate are also the most boring to discuss. Good news though; I'm done with this chapter!

CHAPTER 10

NEGOTIATION SKILLS

Negotiation Basics

When I was around twenty-one years old, I would play board games with friends on occasion. One of my favorites, of course, was Monopoly.

In this classic game, negotiation is part of how it is played. When another player had a property I wanted, I made sure to have something they wanted in return. Either cash or another property was the only thing with which you could negotiate.

After winning in Monopoly several times with the same group of friends, I was treated with contempt by the other players. One player convinced the others not to deal with me, ever. Even if I offered more than what the properties were worth to get a deal done, they wouldn't do it. In effect, I was not allowed to play the game any longer. I was excluded entirely from trading.

I'm not bitter, but I did learn something from the process.

First, taking hard positions in negotiation may win the battle, but you may lose the war. You might get what you want in that circumstance, but later, when it is a bigger deal, or you don't have the strongest position to negotiate, your history with the people involved could destroy your chances of success. This is your reputation, your standing in the community.

Second, I found that sometimes people will negotiate against their own interests if they don't trust you. All the deals I proposed in the game were fair. The other players would have gotten their properties and been that much closer to a monopoly. I just had a better overall strategy than the other players, which led to my winning the game more often.

To keep buying properties and building your real estate empire, you must be skillful at negotiation, the art of the... well, you know (*deal*).

The word *negotiation* is a dirty word to some. It implies that two sides are battling against one another to gain victory over the other. In Spanish, the word for business is *negocio*. The word means dealing with people. It is from the Latin *negotiationem*, business or *negotiari* to carry on business, to do business. In that sense, we as entrepreneurs are negotiating all day, every day.

In real estate, you will have to negotiate when you purchase a property, get the property financed, with contractors to improve the property, and managers who manage the property. As an entrepreneur real estate investor, you need to develop negotiation skills and understand how poor negotiation can hurt you.

If you are successful, sometimes there is a perception that you got there dishonestly. It's unfortunate, but many young people believe what they're told in the media and in universities across the country. The perception that wealth has come on the backs of the poor has been around for a long time. Now, it seems to be more prevalent with the internet, in movies and online streaming shows, and in the twenty-four-hour news cycle.

You should let your integrity speak for itself and cast off all of the stereotypes and judgments that others attempt to label you with.

Be Prepared, and Know What You Want

To be a good negotiator, you need a solid grasp of what you want and a plan as to how you will get there. There are tons of good books on negotiation. I recommend two: *Never Split the Difference: Negotiating as if Your Life Depended On It* by Chris Voss and *Inked: The Ultimate Guide to Powerful Closing and Negotiation Tactics* by Jeb Blount. In some ways, these books contradict each other, but I like the different viewpoints—and the fact that one is coming from a sales point of view and the other is about general negotiation. Both books discuss coming prepared and knowing what your goal is.

Since life is full of negotiations, we often approach business or real estate deals the same way we approach figuring out where we will go for dinner. They, of course, don't have the same impact, and so should be approached differently.

Before a real estate negotiation, take some time to figure out what you want. Write it down. Describe what it looks like and its impact on your real estate portfolio.

On the surface, you may think that you want to negotiate the property's price. In fact, after some thought, your actual goal is to acquire the property at the best price with the least amount of cash out of pocket. With that more precise vision, you'll be able to ask for and concede things that will bring you to that ultimate goal.

In the following sections of this chapter, we'll explore the differences in approach depending on which side of the transaction you are on (buyer versus seller)—and some important and relatively common points about negotiation.

Buyers

How you negotiate depends significantly on whether you're the buyer versus the seller. Both sides have different goals and should use distinct tactics in the negotiation process. Since we're building up your real estate inventory, I'll start with the buyer side.

As a buyer, my goal is to purchase the property at the lowest price possible. Thank you, Captain Obvious! I know; it is breakthrough material here.

As a financial advisor and tax accountant, I've seen people pay ridiculous amounts for what they consider investment property. Then they complain when they aren't making any money on the rents, or when they look to sell the property later.

You make your money in the purchase. Find out how much you can spend on a property to make money by doing your due diligence. What are the rents in that market? What is the price per square foot in that area? What are your financing terms? Asking these questions will help you develop a ceiling price that is the maximum you can spend while still making money. We discussed this in the "Finding and Evaluating Property" chapter.

Now that you have the ceiling, what do you do next? Since most negotiations want you to move upward, you need to give yourself some room to come up to your ceiling. If your ceiling is $100,000, you might come in at $83,172. If the asking price is $125,000, you may not get a response.

It is essential to consider the asking price compared to your ceiling. If the spread is too great, you should probably not make an offer on that property. But, if you are fishing for properties in a market with your investor-centered real estate agent, it is perfectly reasonable to put lowball offers out to several properties to see if the sellers bite. Be prepared for angry real estate agent responses or no response at all.

I'm happy to make these offers, but I know some agents who will not submit them. One of my acquaintances would fill out a contract and take them directly to the sellers' homes to make the offer. They didn't want the agent to sit on the offer or ignore it.

As an investor, sometimes you may be dealing directly with the seller instead of their a real estate agent. I prefer this type of negotiation. It helps me understand what the seller's needs are and what they are willing to concede.

You may notice in the example I shared, I used an uneven number. These types of numbers tell the seller that you have put a lot of thought into your offer and given them the calculated amount that you believe is the property's value. Then, when you begin to negotiate the price, avoid going up in even chunks. If you must counter, do so in small, uneven amounts. Have those amounts prepared before you begin.

There's a great explanation of this process in *Inked* by Jeb Blount. You leave money on the table when you use 5 or 10 percent increments as you move towards your ceiling.

Generally, when I make an offer on a property, I start at around 75 percent of what I believe is the retail market price.

If you remember from our financing discussion, the refinance two-step requires that you purchase the property under 80 percent of fair market value. Starting at 75 percent gives me some room to move to my ceiling.

I once made an offer of 77 percent of appraised value to an investor for a group of properties. He came back with a counter of 75 percent. That's not generally the direction negotiation takes. He wanted to make sure the financing would work for me so he would have money to remodel his house.

Sellers

As the seller—should I say it?—your goal is to get the highest reasonable price for your property. Again with the obvious. Take care, though; whatever sale price you agree on with a buyer, an appraisal will be done and may screw up your deal.

I once contracted to sell a commercial property in a high-traffic area. We had set the list price at around $135,000 and thought that was reasonable. The buyer offered $120,000, and because the property had sat a while, I took it.

But there was a hitch. The appraisal came back at around $105,000, which I couldn't believe. If I'd met that appraiser in a dark alley...

Anyway, the buyer compromised and split the difference with me at $112,500. They had to come up with the additional cash, but they really wanted the property. That is what I mean by *reasonable*. If you set the price beyond retail, only a few buyers have the kind of cash needed to purchase that property. As I type this, I'm sitting in a home that I bought for more than the appraised value. My wife and I also had to make up the difference in cash.

For my residence, I can't blame the appraiser. Sometimes, the market moves so fast upward because of demand that there aren't enough comparable sales that have closed or reported on the multiple listing service (MLS).

As a seller, you must know the market to set a reasonable price. Your real estate agent can pull similar properties that sold in your area and give you a range of prices and the average price per square foot to compare to your property. Setting the price low will get you multiple offers quickly and probably a quick close from the time you put it on the market until the cash hits your account. Setting the price high means you will likely have to wait a while to receive the right offer. If your property sits for too long without any offers or even showings, you may have your home overpriced, and you need to re-evaluate the listing.

Another consideration as the seller is deciding beforehand if you would accept non-conventional financing terms, like seller-financing. There are many reasons to seller-finance a property. You may not want to pay the capital gains taxes on the entire sale all at once. Also, sellers who finance their properties get a higher interest rate than conventional financing. In addition, you generally can sell the property at higher prices than with traditional sales. We talked about seller-financing in the "Making Money in Real Estate" section before. The point here is that you should decide beforehand if this option is on the table.

Making the Offer

There are usually two sets of negotiations in a real estate transaction. First is the agreement on the price. Then there are the seller concessions and possible repairs discovered during the option period.

Sometimes there is a third set of negotiations around the terms, if you ask the seller to finance the property. That will be discussed in the "Seller-Finance Pitch" section of this chapter.

Making an offer is the entry point to all negotiations. Many people put a lot of time and thought into their first offer. While this may be a good strategy for a personal residence, it might not be the best route for commercial or investment property. If you put your best terms in the first offer, you have nowhere to go in the negotiations. Also, since the offer is an entry point, I've found that putting several offers in on several similar properties simultaneously increases my chances of getting the best deal on that type of property.

For instance, I once put ten offers on ten single-family properties of about the same list price and square footage. My offers were well below retail, probably between 60 to 70 percent of the listing price. From those ten offers, two sent back counteroffers. That is when the communication really happens. Those two offers were for 10 to 20 percent less than the listing prices. That told me that the sellers were motivated to sell, and that the real estate agents probably had set the price higher than they were willing to accept.

I call this method of placing offers the *shotgun method*. It has worked well at building my inventory over the years.

One time, I made offers on five different houses at once to five different sellers, only this time they all accepted my offer. I had not expected one of those offers to come back with a counter, much less all five accepting my initial offer. Then I had to scramble to find lenders for the other four houses. Thankfully, we closed on all five homes and increased our cash flow significantly.

I didn't have to close on all five. The offers each had a relatively low escrow amount. So I could have let some or all those contracts go without suffering much of a loss. I could have taken a few of those contracts and pitched them to other investors, taking a finder's fee or, on a simultaneous close, taken the spread, otherwise known as *wholesaling*. (As a reminder, the spread is the difference between what I contracted the house to what I had agreed to sell to other investors.) I love real estate! So many ways to make money! But I really wanted those houses, so I hustled to make them work.

Another consideration is how long the property has been on the market. If it looks like a terrific deal, it doesn't hurt to go ahead and put an offer on it. One of my investor friends used to say, "You don't steal in slow motion!" Deals are out there, and if you find one, don't hesitate to make an offer. Remember that you make your money on the purchase, and the offer is the beginning of the negotiation, not the end.

What Makes a Contract

There are two parts to the *contract*: the offer and the acceptance. These are documented by written agreements, but they can be verbal if witnessed.

Many investors don't realize that a counteroffer nullifies the previous offer. For example, if I offered $100,000 on a property, and the seller countered with $115,000, I'm not bound by, nor can they accept my previous offer. At that point, I would have to accept their counter or counter their counteroffer.

What buyers and sellers should do while they have an offer or counteroffer in hand, is ask, "Would you be willing to accept an offer at…?" This isn't an offer. It is just a question that asks what the other party would be willing to do. If the other party says no, you can still accept the offer you have in hand. This is one of the reasons I prefer to deal directly with sellers, though some real estate agents are very good at feeling the waters of the seller or buyer to determine what price we should put on the offer.

Offers are usually made using boilerplate contracts provided by your state's real estate commission or whatever they call that agency. Creating and editing an offer can be tedious, so knowing what the other party will agree to helps speed up the process.

Seller Concessions

When submitting an offer, you shouldn't be afraid to ask for certain seller concessions. These are normal and expected. What you don't want to do is ask for too much and overdo it, scaring your seller away. You should ask for a home warranty on certain single-family homes.

For example, you should ask for the seller to pay for the survey, or if they have a recent one, to submit it with the other closing documents. I don't like to ask for more than that on investment property. For personal residences, real estate agents often ask the seller to pay half or more of the closing costs. That is fine for FHA financing, but not for investment property.

As an investor, I prefer clean closing statements. I pay for what I am supposed to pay, and the other party pays for what they're supposed to pay. My wife gets so frustrated with homeowners who nitpick every minor thing on the inspection report, at the same time asking us to pay half of their closing costs. We only run into this kind of frustration when we flip houses. I've learned not to tell her the contract details and just stick to bottom-line numbers. It makes for a more peaceful homelife!

Deadlines in Contracts

An important negotiation tool is setting how long the offer is good for. If you give the seller too much time, they will hold onto it, hoping for a better offer to come around. Shortening the time to reply with a counter or acceptance works in your favor. You want to give them enough time to carefully consider your offer, but not too much time for stalling.

Personally, I have a rule: "A hasty decision is a wrong decision." I wouldn't ask a seller to make a hasty decision. I've heard sellers giving someone "until 5:00 p.m. today!" That is pushing the bounds of reason. Three to seven days is plenty of time to make a sound real estate decision for a single-family residence.

Emotional Involvement

Emotions can make you stupid. There, I said it. If you are emotionally attached to any property, it will hurt you on the purchase and the sale.

That said, it happens to the best of us. The first time I walked onto the property at 1211 Kenwood, I was in love. I loved the big back yard, the quaint street, the huge living room, the detached apartment in the back, and the beautiful flower garden along the back fence. I told the owner I wanted it before we ever stepped inside. I don't know what came over me, really. If I'd had my investor mind that day, I would have noticed it only had a one-car driveway that would be very frustrating later. Or that the walls upstairs weren't plum. After thousands of dollars in remodeling, and a few weeks living in one of our investment properties, I finally saw that it wasn't as great as I'd first thought. It was a good house, and my wife loved it.

What upsets me most is that I didn't even negotiate with the seller. Emotion took over, and we left money on the table. Since then, I've done well to keep emotion out of our real estate purchases. The cost of emotional purchase in real estate is high.

Seller-Financing Pitch

One negotiating tool is the *seller-financing* pitch. After you determine what the seller wants, you give them everything they want with the condition that they will give you your terms.

As mentioned before, making the offer starts the conversation. The seller responds with a counteroffer of, presumably, their target sale price. Then you say, "If I give you the full price, will you finance the property on my terms?" You can do this, because you are not emotionally involved and already have financing prepared if the seller isn't willing to finance the deal.

What might motivate a seller to be the lender? First, seller-financing creates an installment note. These transactions have special tax treatment that allows the seller to spread the tax over the term of the note. Second, the interest rates the buyer pays are usually better than most other investments. Some sellers finance at rates all the way up to 10 percent. As a seller, I usually ask a borrower to pay two times what I would pay for that mortgage. For example, if my cost to borrow is 3.25 percent, I would ask the borrower to pay 6.5 percent.

Additionally, if you must repossess the property as the seller-financer, as long as there aren't major repairs or renovations, you get to keep the down payment money and start the process all over again. If this happens several years after the initial sale, the appreciation on the property might be substantial.

We don't ever want to take back a property from a tenant. As we have stated before, we don't set them up to fail.

The seller's benefits to this setup are real and should overcome most objections, except the big one: The seller has already spent the cash in their mind. If the seller has plans for the money or is doing a 1031 exchange, the buyer will just have to move on or get it financed traditionally.

A 1031 exchange refers to the IRS tax code, section 1031. The details are beyond the scope of this book, but this code section allows a seller to defer taxation on the sale of the property if they use the proceeds in the purchase of a similar or "like-kind" property. It is also referred to as a *Like-Kind* exchange. The replacement property must be located within forty-five days of the sale of the original property and subsequently, the sale closed within 180 days of the original sale date.

What is the benefit of seller-financing to you, if you are the buyer? Mostly, it is an easier closing experience. Financial institutions have tons of attorneys that create all kinds of hoops to jump through. Most seller-financed transactions happen quickly and are self-closed. You might have your attorney review the documents before you sign them, but it isn't as complicated as banks and mortgage companies make it. Even the seller-financed closings that happen at a title company are much faster and have fewer documents to wade through. And usually the down payment requirement is less.

The combination of a quick close and low down is very attractive to investors—especially if you can refinance within twelve months to reduce the interest rate to a more competitive rate. Be sure to ask about prepayment penalties. Some real estate liens (notes) have a clause that charges you percentage points (points) if you pay off the note too fast. It isn't a deal breaker if this is included in the documents; you just need to know if it is there and make an informed decision.

The seller-finance pitch negotiation tool is one that not many people pursue. I am of the mindset that "you have not, because you ask not." If you don't ask to see if they are willing to seller-finance, you may be using more cash than necessary.

CHAPTER 11

CONCLUSION

This Stuff Works

Another of my clients, we'll call him Tony, was the owner of a small restaurant in San Angelo, Texas. After a few years of struggling, he began to see a level of success that created excess cash in his business. He came to me and asked questions about real estate and how I got started. We talked on a regular basis about many of the principles in this book.

Over time, he has put those principles to work to build his real estate empire. As a smart entrepreneur and real estate investor, he also gained relationships with other investors, bankers, real estate agents, and attorneys. I can't say that it was through my guidance alone, but I can say I had a significant input in his real estate journey. He has now increased his holdings to over ten properties.

Recently, Tony began offering remodel services on the side. The remodel crew members he uses on his own properties are now available to work on other projects, which helps them keep their jobs.

I am very proud of what he has accomplished. There are new businesses and much more real estate on the horizon for him.

I know the principles in this book will help you build your real estate portfolio as well. They have worked for me and for those I have coached in real estate investing.

What You've Learned

We explored knowing the various ways to make money in real estate, so you can pick the revenue stream that works best for you. There are several money-making avenues to take in real estate. From "fix and flip," "buy, rehab, and rent," to "buy, rehab, and seller-finance," and many others. Find the one you feel most comfortable with, and begin your investing career.

Gathering a team of advisors around you will help you make the most of your capital. This team should include a coach or mentor, a real estate agent, an enlightened CPA, a banker and a real estate attorney. It may take a while fill all the seats, but it is worth it to find the right team members for the journey.

With an entrepreneur mindset, guided by your vision, mission and values, set goals for yourself and see those goals become reality. This mindset creates policies and procedures for how you operate and determines the strategies you employ to reach your goals. Running your real estate investing like a business keeps you focused.

You can become an expert in your market and find properties that fit your investing model—meeting the criteria you set before you began looking for that perfect property. Using a real estate agent to find properties can be your best source, but there are other ways to find them. FSBOs, foreclosures, other investors can also be great pipelines for your real estate empire.

Financing your property can take on many faces. Traditional conventional financing is not the only method. Learn what programs are available at the banks in your area, and use some of the options we discussed. We had tons of banks tell us *no*, until one told us *yes*. It only takes one. If the bank won't finance the property you want, maybe the seller will—or maybe a hard money lender or group of other investors. Be creative when financing your deal.

Once purchased, you will have to manage your income-producing property. Either by yourself or by hiring a professional, you now know what to look for, and how to set up processes and procedures to make your life easier.

You also know that not all opportunities are opportunities for you. Be diligent to pursue those that meet your criteria and business model, but don't be afraid to learn something new. Try different investing models in small doses before committing to one type of revenue stream. Whatever stream you choose, become an expert before you move on to the next model. Even when choosing a new model, stick to what you know. If you don't know anything about it, you can educate yourself with books, podcasts, coaches, and your team.

As you pick up steam and add properties, you will need to think about how you will protect those properties from creditors and taxes. The form of ownership is the first stage of asset protection. Work with your CPA and attorney to decide what is best for you.

Lastly, we talked about developing your negotiation skills; knowing what you want and developing a plan to get there. Having your price points set before you get to the negotiation table is imperative. These skills are developed over time, and even the experienced investors fail occasionally. Each experience is an opportunity to learn and build your skill set.

What's Next For You?

Why did you read this book? You finished it, so something about it stirred up some call to action inside you. What is that call telling you right now?

I don't know if you read the Bible much, but the story about the plagues of Egypt is pretty well-known. Moses is told to go to Egypt to rescue the children of Israel and is met with pretty strong resistance.

One of the nine plagues used was the overwhelming presence of frogs. They were everywhere, in everything. Pharaoh, the ruler of Egypt, called Moses into his court and asked Moses to remove the frogs. Moses responds by saying, "I leave to you the honor of setting the time for me to pray for you and your officials and your people that you and your houses may be rid of the frogs, except for those that remain in the Nile" (Exodus 8:9). So what does Pharaoh say? *Tomorrow!*

You may not be a Christian or Jewish, but that is a very interesting response. *When do you want the pain to go away? When do you want things to change?* It is a common response. "I'll do something about this tomorrow." Then tomorrow never comes.

Why not today? Why don't you begin your real estate journey today?

If you need some help, there are plenty of investors who would be willing to give you a hand. We've talked some about the mentor and coach. One of their main jobs is to help keep you accountable to your plan. We all need someone on our side who will get on our case if we start to wander off the road.

Likewise, use this book as the roadmap that it is. Don't let it sit on your shelf or in your digital library as one of those *good books you read once*. Move forward from here. Take a step towards making real estate part of your life.

If you would like to be on my mailing list to receive ongoing tips, please go to my website and sign up there. You can reach out for business or real estate coaching from my website www. brandonkmoore.com as well as by emailing me. Please give me a review of the book and let me know what other information might be helpful. Also, check out my podcast "Coaching for Profit" on Spotify or wherever you enjoy podcasts.

ABOUT THE AUTHOR

 Brandon Moore is a CPA, Certified Wealth Strategist©, coach, and real estate investor who has successfully purchased and managed more than one hundred residences—while equipping others to thrive in reaching their financial goals. Like many successful entrepreneurs, however, Brandon's career path hasn't been direct. The curves in his route have defined his success—while deepening his expertise.

Brandon didn't graduate at the top of his high school class. Instead, he lost his only run at student council, and a bout of pneumonia gave him an early (and perhaps fortuitous) opportunity to drop out of college (without grief from his father, he says).

After working as a janitor, losing a job as a life insurance agent, and serving as church youth director and eventually bookkeeper, Brandon decided to pursue a new career: that of an accountant.

Brandon then graduated from Angelo State University and began investing in real estate—buying two houses with no money down. A few years later, he acquired his CPA designation, and at age thirty-one, bought his first CPA firm—while building his real estate empire. Later, he purchased another four accounting practices. And during the 2008 recession, he acquired his financial service licenses to better serve CPA clients. He passed the Series 7, Series 66, and Life Insurance Agents license tests and has consistently remained in the top five to ten advisors of his broker/dealer.

Today, Brandon advises clients on wealth management—including charitable giving, estate planning, tax planning, retirement planning, investment allocation, risk management, and more. Brandon and his wife of twenty-five years, Angela, invest in and manage single-family properties and duplexes in West Texas—once acquiring thirty-three properties in one purchase. They have four children, who have been involved in the real estate business from early on.

Beyond the certifications and accolades, Brandon believes his purpose is to coach and develop leaders. He wants his family, friends, and clients to become their best selves, which is why he writes books and runs his podcast, "Coaching for Profit." He says, "I may only be able to coach a handful of people per day, week, or month. But these books can reach people exponentially."

In his free time, Brandon loves music and plays multiple instruments—often in his church. Brandon also recently reached his goal of third-degree black belt in Taekwondo, believing that martial arts offer a continuous improvement philosophy—training both mind and body.

For all of his experience and interests, Brandon has closets full of awards that he doesn't display, because as he states, "It is because of my clients that I have done well. They are such a blessing to work with and for." Connect with Brandon at www. brandonkmoore.com.

Made in United States
Orlando, FL
22 March 2022

16059050R00096